The Roving I

Collected columns, wit, wisdom, and self-exposure of Woody Weingarten

Author of *Rollercoaster: How a man can survive his partner's breast cancer* and *Grampy and His Fairyzona Playmates*

Across the U.S. *and* the globe, readers hail *The Roving I*

"Woody Weingarten brings the sharpest of eyes and keenest of ears to this bracing collection of his newspaper columns. No subject, large or small, escapes his powers of observation and instinct for getting to the heart of the matter. Whether recounting the simple joys of grandparenting, a harrowing Holocaust survivor's tale, or cataloguing the best of eavesdropped conversations in the mall, he remains first and foremost a reporter of unflinching honesty and inerrant lyrical style."
— Dan Pine; Albany, California

"Beautifully written with cleverness and empathy, *The Roving* I exhibits a wide array of very readable stories taken from real life — from celebrations to births to deaths to pets and everything in between. You will chuckle, you might cry, but you will definitely relate to these enjoyable bite-sized essays."
— Arlene Miller, The Grammar Diva, Best-selling author, blogger, and speaker; Tampa, Florida

"*The Roving I* is like hanging out at a small-town coffee shop and meeting the locals through the guy who knows them all personally. Personable and delightful!"
— Becky Parker Geist; Portland, Oregon

"Woody Weingarten's wordsmithing is crafted from experience and passion and is as interesting as it is entertaining. His book is filled with fascinating vignettes that show humour, compassionate sadness, and life messages worth reading. The author provides a diverse compilation of short stories on people, animals, love, tolerance, and empathy while conveying a wise mindfulness of life and life's journey."
— Peter Harris; Melbourne, Australia

"These quick-to-read introductions to all sorts of characters and topics brought a smile to my mood. I felt as if I'd been to a party where I met a bunch of great characters. Treat yourself and dive into this snappy, upbeat collection filled with quips and wordplay. You won't be sorry."
— Sara Becker; Moraga, California

"Like my experience with *The Squid Game*, which I binge-watched in one weekend, I just binge-read all the columns in *The Roving I* and loved every single one. The author makes words — and his observations — come alive."
— Ann Israel; Hudson, New York

"In *The Roving I,* the author treats us to his collection of keen, candid, heart-warming stories reflecting his compassionate views, with a gentle sense of humor and an occasional touch of irony, on all the memorable, and sometimes not-so-memorable, events and foibles that make life so special. Long after closing the cover, I find some vignettes still resonate in unexpected ways."
— Jeff Nebenzahl; Mill Valley, California

"The writer's essays in *The Roving I* pulse with brio, insight, and humor. He is an amusing, bright-eyed chronicler of people and places, known and unknown."
— Fayette Hickox; Weston, Connecticut

"Woody Weingarten's columns are warm, witty, thoughtful, and charming, much like the man himself."
— Michael Rosenthal; Fairfax, California

"Hot on the heels of the award-winning *Grampy and His Fairzona Playmates*, a collaboration with his granddaughter, Hannah Schifrin, *The Roving I* is exactly what Woody Weingarten hoped it would be — a labor of love. Culled from a decade of essays penned for weekly newspapers, the author's pleasure in a life well-lived jumps off the page. An antidote to the ugliness all around us."
— Terrance Gelenter, *The Paris Insider* newsletter; Paris, France

"Woody Weingarten's work reflects the finely tuned ear and observant eye of a career journalist. But these columns reflect more than reporting: They capture an American Odyssey in the promise of New York, the counterculture of California, the love of a father and grandfather, the devotion of a husband. Full of wit and wordplay, *The Roving I* reveals a wordsmith who welcomes, and questions, everything."
— Alex Orquiza, Associate Professor, History and Classics, Providence College; Providence, Rhode Island

"This collection of essays is brilliant! I say this because Woody Weingarten has the rare capacity to connect with readers through humor and thoughtful analysis simultaneously. This is no small feat, and this collection can be compared to Mark Twain's pithy humor, which camouflages the depth and seriousness of his subject matter. For example, writing about the death of a dear friend named David, the writer says: "On his deathbed, my psychologist/consultant pal, still boyishly good-looking despite being sixty-something, and still a pigheaded St. Louis Cardinals fanatic, revisited his spiritual feelings." The author's reference to David's fanaticism about the Cardinals expresses more about the jokey, intimate nature of their friendship than any narrative could. And it also poignantly clarifies how much David's absence will be felt. Every essay in this collection is spiced with jokes, puns, hilarious observations, deep compassion, and eternal truths. Get this book! It's deeply satisfying on every level."
— Fiona Quinn; Chicago, Illinois

"Great insight and eloquence comes easy, or appears to, in these essays. Be entertained while learning and being inspired."
— Joaquin Marques; Barcelona, Spain

"Humor and humanity are laced throughout this anthology, a delicious smorgasbord of light-hearted observations interspersed with soul-quenching vignettes. The author focuses on a kaleidoscope of colorful characters and generously shares pieces of his life, which has been so graced with great love."
— Lindsey McLorg; San Anselmo, California

"'Human interest' isn't quite the term for Woody Weingarten's genre — 'human fascination' is closer. He makes a sublime meal out of the material of real people's lives, whether he's celebrating the first words of a friend's child or weaving hilarious poetry out of overheard snippets from a day's errands. In a media ecosystem full of negativity and instability writ large, his fly-on-the-wall and first-hand stories from around the corner or across the world are a breath of fresh air. On the human scale, there is so much to be excited about! And why shouldn't the county fair be featured? Or a Thanksgiving meal for seniors in need? At the heart of the author's fascination is his clear love for humanity. So, who better to write about it?"
— Avery Bargar; Brooklyn, New York

"Woody Weingarten uses his amazing writing talent to tell unique stories that are inciteful, entertaining, and informative. He creatively brings forth the essence of his narrative with wit, wonderment, and wisdom. The stories in *The Roving I* demonstrate that he has a knack for telling a tale you want to hear. His book is delightful and fun to read."
— Gloria Dunn-Violin, Author of *Revivement* and *Wiser Ways to Work*; Novato, California

"Woody Weingarten handles every subject in this collection with a gentle touch and sometimes a mischievous wink. His short articles, in effect a guide to good news and small joys, help remind me of my life in Northern California before moving to Mexico several years ago."
— Rhoda Draws; San Miguel de Allende, Mexico

"*The Roving I* is a great, fun, poignant read. Bravo!"
— David Landis, *The Gay Gourmet* columnist; San Francisco, California

"A warm, human-hearted read — *meticulous, generous, and loving* — mirroring the author himself, a curious, kindhearted, adventuresome man who pictures for us the lives of the many he met, loved, and loves. Just the kind of read we need, especially these days."
— Michael Scott; Sausalito, California

"Woody Weingarten is an optimist who mindfully sees and shares the good news expressed by others. He's also a realist whose enthusiasm for living in our kaleidoscopic universe is catching. He raises my spirit when he writes of the varieties of human experience: A refugee from Cambodia's Maoist Khmer Rouge, a school janitor, a bus driver, the homeless, and the hungry. *The Roving I* is ecumenical, sometimes as personal as his lifelong adoration of his wife — as well as his lifelong appreciation of other women who catch his eye. The writer not only counts his lucky stars but his blessings: "Aging is an amazing process: As my hearing has decreased, my listening has increased; as my eyesight has blurred, my insights have sharpened." He brightens my day."
— Lance Woodruff; Philadelphia, Pennsylvania

Collected columns, wit, wisdom,
and self-exposure of Woody Weingarten

Author of *Rollercoaster: How a man can survive his partner's breast cancer* and *Grampy and His Fairyzona Playmates*

VitalityPress

VitalityPress
VitalityPress.com

Publishing management by Ruth Schwartz, thewonderlady.com
Cover design: Joe Marciniak
Back cover photo: Alan Babbitt

Publisher's Cataloging-in-Publication data

Names: Weingarten, Woody, author.
Title: The roving I : collected columns, wit, wisdom, and self-exposure of Woody Weingarten / Woody Weingarten.
Description: San Anselmo, CA: VitalityPress, 2022.
Identifiers: LCCN: 2022915921 | ISBN: 978-0-9905543-8-7 (hardcover) | 978-0-9905543-6-3 (paperback) | 978-0-9905543-7-0 (ebook)
Subjects: LCSH Weingarten, Woody. | Essays. | Humor. | BISAC BIOGRAPHY & AUTOBIOGRAPHY / Editors, Journalists, Publishers | BIOGRAPHY & AUTOBIOGRAPHY / Personal Memoirs | HUMOR / Form / Essays
Classification: LCC PN4874 .W45 2022 | DDC 071.9/092--dc23

Dedication and thanks

This book is dedicated with tenderness and affection to Nancy Fox, my wife and soulmate; Janis Brown and Mark Weingarten, my daughter and son; Drew Brown, Zachary Weingarten and Hannah Schifrin, my grandchildren — all of whom have consistently given me love and admiration even when I handed them spurts of temper or inflexibility.

I offer thanks, too, to Joe Marciniak, who took my concept for this book's front cover and executed it perfectly as a cartoon; and to Alan Babbitt, whose back-cover photograph still captures Nancy and me lovingly staring at each other.

I'm also grateful for all those folks who opened up when I interviewed them, enabling me to craft columns that readers might relate to and enjoy.

Woody Weingarten
San Anselmo, California
September 25, 2022

Table of Contents

Part 1 — An introduction by the author 1

Part 2 — Uncommon friends 5

'Miracle baby' walks, talks, and inspires euphoria 7

Parkinson's disease can't shake un-still photographer's grit............ 11

A tale of two women's survival — and apes and elephants 15

Compassion overrides resistance to rescuing countless dogs 19

Hairstylist to the stars now honing his acting chops 23

He's gone from coloring book to colorful views of candidates .. 27

Sportscaster turns his surfing into waves of therapy 31

When a buddy dies, it's time to mourn — and to change............. 35

Part 3 — Family sketches 39

She's playful, opinionated, cautious, loving — and four................ 41

My little girl turns 50, with unforeseen touches of high drama..... 45

My son's hip surgery thrusts me into a tricky role.......................... 49

Robin Williams becomes the icing on family-vacation cake 53

I celebrate my dog's life — and simultaneously taste mortality 57

Part 4 — Quickie insights 61

Humor, wisdom, pathos — all are within earshot 63

I chew and chew on overheard chit-chat 67

Selfie-ing, snooping, swearing — etc., etc., etc., and so forth 71

Post-its help me vent, amuse, and flaunt my ignorance 75

Post-its redux: fresh looks at joy, irritation, nonsense..................... 79

Snippets of conversations beguile, titillate, and shock 83

Phony-baloney items? Nope — funny, touching, odd eavesdroppings 87

Part 5 — Human rareties 91

Cambodian refugee works her dream after surviving slave-labor camp 93

What's possible? Just ask the developmentally disabled dynamo 97

Nonagenarian spearheads tributes to Rosie the Riveter 101

Two feed the hungry, differently, as their hearts ache 105

Two women who resisted the Nazis will never forget 109

Un-ordinary Joe pushes poetry, combats bullying 113

Real men *do* cry — tears that might fend off violence 117

Part 6 — Natural wonders 121

Writer witnesses woodsy, weird, whimsical wildlife 123

To bee or not to bee, I learned to mingle with 5,000 of them 127

I find beauty in what surrounds me — instead of disasters 131

Ready to trade in my gas-guzzler to save the planet? Not yet 135

Finding visible beauty instead of invisible men 139

Part 7 — Amazing wife 143

White keys, black keys, nostalgia, and magic 145

Overcoming both hearing loss and bullying 149

My wife and I prefer not to think about everything we've lost 153

Getting the hang of living happily ever after 157

Part 8 — She 'n' me 161

Joint sickbed becomes a hotbed for blessings 163

Zanzibar? Staycation features imaginary flight there 167

I'm a caring husband but I'm in alien territory 171

Part 9 — This 'n' that 175

Little Black Book stirs memories of lovers, relocations, true love. 177

Stupid, klutzy, human — yeah, all those labels fit me 181

How I overcame a particularly troublesome week........................ 185

Duck, parakeets, Schnauzer spur elder-facility joy 189

Safe from storms, I bleed for the homeless who aren't................. 193

I peek into a crystal ball and eye being a centenarian 197

'Hidden' café draws a diverse, cheerful lunch bunch 201

Part 10 — More rarities.. 205

'Riding shotgun' on a recycling truck can be a delight................. 207

Protester-artist playfully jabs at toxins in society 211

He's collected 75,000 pieces of stuff — a definite 'wow' 215

Four floods and 65 years later, he's still cutting hair..................... 219

Founder of co-op repairs bikes and the environment.................. 223

Working mom wants to run every street in the county 227

Aging doesn't abrogate work of lawyer who aids underdogs........ 231

Stroke survivor exemplifies courageous, upbeat attitude.............. 235

Part 11 — Indelible instances 239

At 75, I wish for everything — except world peace...................... 241

Media disrespect the good work of teenagers 245

Auto-erratic behavior — a what-*not*-to-do list 249

Counting my lucky stars — and my blessings 253

Part 12 — More this 'n' that 257

The verdict's in — despite imperfections, juries work 259

Buses offer less stress, a bargain, and a chance to snooze............. 263

'Invisible,' jolly custodians keep high school spotless 267

Hoping for a permanent job seasonally bell ringing 271
The village that aids older adults can do almost anything 275
Is art whatever you foist on an unsuspecting public? 279
Those who are helping homeless youth need our help 283
Breast cancer awareness should transcend pink ribbons 287

Part 13 — Ego-tripping 291

Is my entire life just one big gamble? 293
Ego-tripping leaves zero time for 'retirement' 297
My scaredy-cat fears: big cougars, little bugs 301
Do-Nothing Day turns into a full-fledged fiasco 305

Short autobiography of the author 309

Part 1
An introduction by the author

This book is exactly what I'd hoped it would be — a labor of love.

For nearly a dozen years, I regularly wrote first-person essays under the rubric *The Roving I* for half a dozen weekly newspapers in Marin County, a locale I adore despite having impertinently described it as one traffic jam north of the Golden Gate Bridge.

Minor editing has deleted most of the repetition and shifted the focus of the *Marinscope* columns from small-town California to universality. I've culled a healthy sampling — 70 of my favorites — for this anthology. Many are lighthearted; a handful are weighty.

More than a few, however, may be frozen in time. My wife's signature flowing red hair, for instance, has turned into a white bob. Everyone else referred to, including me, has also aged (or, in one case, died). Some have married, divorced, moved, changed jobs; some organizations have rebranded themselves.

None of that affects the merits or impact of the columns, however.

You can still read how my attempt to do *nothing* became an instant fiasco, how a photographer turned his Parkinson's disease into an asset, how a Cambodian slave-labor camp escapee became a successful U.S. entrepreneur, how my bewitching partner earned a slot in my Little Black Book, and how a guy who styled the hair of Alice Cooper, Billy Idol, and Eric Clapton left Los Angeles after deciding you can live there only if you're "young, good-looking, or both."

You can check out, too, stories that detail how one sister carried another's "miracle baby" inside her for the requisite nine months, how eavesdropping let me share a bicyclist's view that her boyfriend "was feral" when she first met him, and how Robin Williams transformed himself into a talking vagina.

The compilation in your hand also includes a re-telling of how happy a pet duck made residents of an assisted living facility, and how the loss of a buddy who left behind a lengthy string of wives, girlfriends, and broken hearts spurred me to continue fighting for the environment, the homeless, and equal rights.

I hope you'll enjoy dipping into these vintage first-person memories as much as I did when I created them.

Part 2
Uncommon friends

'Miracle baby' walks, talks, and inspires euphoria

The "miracle baby" turns one on March 9. Abigail Sander's first birthday will be a celebration of life — and scientific marvels.

Her family will also pay homage to those who survived the Holocaust, and those who didn't.

Festivities will effervesce at a party in Brooklyn, where Abi lives with her mom and dad, Heidi and Jeremy, and giggles liberally. Later she'll be the focus of another bash — in Marin County, California, where she lived nine months in utero, in the bulging surrogate belly of Heidi's older sister, Alaina Yoakum.

How do I fit in? The sisters insist my wife and I, friends but unrelated, are part of their extended family. So, I'll hoist the kid onto my lap at that shindig and, for the fourth time since her birth, revel in her chuckles.

"I can lose myself in just staring at her," Heidi said recently. I can, too — because I know what it took for Abi to get here.

Antecedents include Heidi's cervical cancer four years ago at age 28, a hysterectomy, freezing her eggs after Jeremy fertilized them, psychological screenings and lab tests, a costly surrogacy, and expensive legal paperwork.

For Alaina, past-40 co-owner with husband, Charles, of Marin Running Company in San Anselmo, my adopted hometown, it wasn't an easy pregnancy. Shots to prevent premature birth. Copious mood swings. Headaches. Elevated blood pressure.

Earlier, fear for Heidi's life hounded her parents. Because Ivan Silverberg, the sisters' dad, is an oncologist, and their mom, Rita Rosenbaum, an oncology nurse, both agonized during the cancer treatments. They imagined everything that could go wrong.

Thankfully, nothing did.

Rita now reminisces about "how strong Heidi was, how resilient she was, how she handled it all." She lauds, too, Alaina's lovingkindness, Jeremy's attentiveness, and Charles' support (including, for months, giving Alaina daily injections of progesterone). Ivan echoes that, but grumbles about being "a two-coast family" and not seeing "Abi enough, even though Heidi's gone out of her way to get here."

The Brooklynites actually expect to juggle jobs, friends and calendars to bring Abigail here every other month.

That'll help the family concentrate on what's good — and mollify Rita's dark memories. Her father was the only member of his family to survive the Holocaust; her mother's family was likewise decimated.

How many died? "Too many to count," she tells me, explaining that for her, a child of survivors, the residue was "distrust — of the world, the government, the police, neighbors and friends. I knew no matter how good everything looked today, it could be taken away tomorrow."

But the presence of Abigail, named after two Abrahams, Rita's and Ivan's dads, helps her relax a little — as do the Yoakum daughters, Sophie and Olivia. That duo bolstered the cheerfulness in San Francisco's Kaiser Permanente when Abi emerged after the C-section. "They were so much a part of this," recalls Rita. "They laughed, quietly, with sheer delight."

Delight also was the operative word when Alaina, who's "always had this incredible bond" with Heidi despite their 10-year age difference and who chats "with her almost daily by phone and online," asked to stand in.

Amazingly, Charles dreamt her surrogacy the night before (though his subconscious got the kid's gender wrong).

Only one egg had to be implanted. That leaves about a dozen should Heidi someday decide she fancies a gigantic family. For now, though, she has her hands full with Abi, who already has a love-filled history that, for me, began with welcome-to-the-world merrymaking at Rita and Ivan's place in Mill Valley (where Heidi, Alaina and their brother Michael grew up). My eyes misted while cradling her.

Later, during the baby-naming ritual at Congregation Kol Shofar, a morning of wonder and tenderness as mother and surrogate chanted together, my tear ducts leaked freely. Then, when Abi hit three months, I held her for 40 straight, glorious minutes. She cooed and clutched my finger. I cooed back.

In October, at the Yoakum's place, I again cradled her. She grabbed my finger as if remembering the other time. I kvelled. That's a Yiddish word that means being elated. Euphoric.

What will Abigail call Alaina? "Neither mommy nor auntie are quite right. We've agreed to wait and see what nickname she comes up with," explains Heidi. Alaina concurs.

Abi walks now, warbles a few words, and gets ecstatic playing peek-a-boo. "She also giggles at other babies," Heidi reports, "and she likes to look at pictures of herself in my cellphone."

None of that's unusual. But some still think everything concerning the "miracle baby" is unique.

Heidi views it differently: "Abigail is certainly a miracle for us, but we feel a little uncomfortable calling her that because any baby could be given that label."

True, but I still see Heidi being played by Natalie Portman in a short black wig, Alaina by a brunette Scarlett Johansson. Abi, I figure, will star as the miracle kid.

Parkinson's disease can't shake un-still photographer's grit

It's a paradox: Alan Babbitt doesn't see well. But his vision is sharper than most.

The 61-year-old is succinct: "I was born with a whole bunch of eye problems, so I was wearing thick glasses from the age of 2 or 3. There's no question — without contacts, I'd be legally blind."

He refused to let the impairment get in his way, however. It certainly didn't block his becoming a successful film and video producer, webmaster, and award-winning photographer.

Alan used his website to exhibit his skill. One portfolio spotlighted the Santa Cruz boardwalk on a winter's day. Another contained dramatic, artsy New York City street scenes. A third focused on playful images. Showcased were unusual angles and perspectives, brilliant colors, and poignant black-and-white shots.

His originality makes the scenically difficult look easy to capture. And he loves peppering his explanatory text with dubious puns and any remnants of humor that happen to be lying around. For example, he confesses that he once "joined a therapy group for photo addicts based on the '12-Stop program.'"

Unfortunately, Parkinson's disease invaded his life five years ago "like a loud, uninvited house guest who won't ever leave." The physical shaking made him totally reexamine his life — and shelf his camera for a while.

Now, my friend and I sit in a quiet Thai restaurant enjoying the sunshine streaming through the windows. He beams, almost mischievously, like a kid about to let me in on a gigantic secret. "Parkinson's *adds* to my vision," he says. "Recognizing I could use the tremor freed me up like nothing else."

I need no follow-up question; he's on a roll.

"The disease is about losing control. Finding I could use it was empowering.

"When you first learn photography, they tell you over and over about crispness, about keeping the camera steady with a tripod. One evening in Las Vegas, where I was alone with a digital camera, I just started shooting. I was able to see right away what I got. Blurs. Streaks. And then people started reacting to it, liking it. That's my style now — tremor-enhanced photography."

His website contained portfolios dedicated to his innovative technique, "Movement Disorder" and "Shake Me Out to the Ball Game."

He beams again as he chats about "crossing the border" and journeying to metaphoric "other lands" through his camera lens — speeding past his disability: "The tremor is only one kind of movement. I can shoot from a moving car and move the camera around as well. It's sort of what I call 'un-still photography.'"

He, too, is un-still.

Alan's taught at the de Young Museum Art School in San Francisco, exhibited at galleries and studios, held shows at libraries here and there in California and Washington state. He's planning an April exhibit of his photos at the public library in his hometown, Fairfax — to mark National Parkinson's Month.

He's also contacted the Michael J. Fox Foundation to see if they can work together. He's donated prints to a Parkinson's group in New York, his birth state, to be auctioned off, and to another foundation. And he recently participated in an Art for Recovery program in San Francisco featuring readings from letters exchanged by patients and medical students.

"One of the gratifying things is that people have seen the work and been inspired by what I'm doing," he tells me. "It feels good getting those e-mails and letters. Some of them have been from photographers. And a 12-year-old girl wrote me the other day and asked to use me as the basis of a school report. That's the kind of thing that inspires me to do more."

Still, it can feel pretty heavy — until you fully grasp the positive attitude that gushes from the bearded, gray-haired guy with brown eyes.

There's no doubt Alan cultivates his tendency to be upbeat, his affinity for the amusing, readily admitting he wants viewers to relish their "titters, snickers, and snorts."

"Soon after I got the diagnosis," he recalls, "I thought of occupations that would be possible by using tremors: egg-scrambler, paint can-shaker, human vibrator. Sure, having Parkinson's can be depressing, but humor can help fight that."

His occasionally dark humor was quickly evident online, sprinkled between his straightforward photos and experimental tremor-shots that highlighted bright streaks and patches, rings and blotches of light, geometric shapes.

Spoofing a Viagra ad, he warns that "if feelings of giddiness…persist for more than four hours, just turn on the news for a few minutes."

A tale of two women's survival – and apes and elephants

Carol Keys and Linda Albion are breast cancer survivors.

Both are 67. Both are my Northern California friends, a perk from their attachment to my wife, another longtime survivor of the disease. And both not only are concerned with women battling breast cancer but with animals at risk of extinction — apes and elephants, specifically.

Carol first became interested in simians in the '60s "when the first language work with them — sentient beings who could learn and communicate with us in *our* languages — was being published."

Back then, she tells me, she knew of "no humans who could 'speak ape,' though now I know lots of people fluent in ape languages — and I'm fluent in chimpanzee."

The redhead studied the primates' plight and "decided I had to do something. So, I spent a month in East Africa and had close encounters with gorillas and chimpanzees." Eventually she found herself traveling to a different sanctuary every year, and co-founding a volunteer animal welfare and conservation organization, the Pan-African Sanctuary Alliance (PASA), which helps ape sanctuaries communicate with each other.

Carol, who's worked with it 15 years (including as board chair), helped PASA — now in 13 countries and linked with primatologist Jane Goodall — raise money. Why? "Apes, our closest genetic cousins, are in trouble because of habitat destruction, illegal pet trade, and illegal hunting."

What she says underscores what my buddy Bernie Krause, ecologist and sound expert who also worked with Goodall, has told me repeatedly. Carol's just a touch less scientific about it — especially when she relates how Pasa, orphan chimp named after the organization, stole her heart at the Ngamba Island Sanctuary in Uganda.

"I was so in love with this baby, who took a bottle every couple of hours, who snuggled into me, who was developmentally identical to any human baby, as they all are for their first two years.

"I was supposed to leave after a week, but I prolonged my trip. When I finally left, Pasa transferred well to her new 'mommy.' I didn't do so well. I left with a broken heart."

Linda, a dirty blonde who came to Marin County in '71, can also get worked up about saving mammals. Particularly pachyderms. An elephant conservancy in Thailand, near Chaing Mai helped shape her feelings.

Both African and Asian elephants "might disappear in our children's lifetimes," she asserts. "We absolutely must have sanctuaries and conservancies."

What piqued her interest? "I flew for PanAm — when they called us stewardesses — and saw animals all around the world. Elephants were a big part of my draw to Africa 'cause they're so intelligent, so gentle, so evolved. But it's a conundrum: How do we find the food and space for all of them?"

One answer, she suggests, is tourism. "I've been to the conservancy three times. I'd spend a week, from 6:30 in the morning to late afternoon, learning how the elephants behave, how they think, how they live, and how they respond to their mahouts, their trainers. We'd bathe the elephants twice a day because they like it, and we'd see how much they play with each other. We'd show tourists what *we* were learning."

Linda's environmental interests extend to keeping bees, which "are in peril too, because of pesticides and monoculture."

Less seriously, she talks about a fly that's been in her car three weeks — despite her opening windows for its escape. She's named it Jeff.

Both women became interested in critters as kids.

When Carol was a toddler, her grandmother "had many cats. I couldn't keep my hands off them. And I thought every neighbor's dog was mine. Then the Easter Bunny left me a tiny German Shepherd puppy when I was three."

Linda's animal fixation stretches even further — "to before I could walk. I had a nanny that was a dog, Penny, a Collie."

But protecting critters needn't date from childhood. My wife — in a breast-cancer support group with Linda more than 20 years and the heroine of my book, *Rollercoaster: How a man can survive his partner's breast cancer* — didn't become education director of the Marin Humane Society until her 40s. Clearly, adulthood's not too late.

Both Carol and Linda are thoroughly enjoying post-cancer lives. Linda connects the dots: "I wish I had some brilliant quote about surviving this world. I don't. But we need to be in tune with nature and whatever nature can give us. Oh, I've got it: 'Nobody survives alone.'"

Compassion overrides resistance to rescuing countless dogs

Patrice Hickox may be a dog-adoption parallel to Angelina Jolie.

Angelina, a Hollywood sexpot, has augmented her fame by rearing kids of various heritages and skin colors; Hickox, a Fairfax resident in an analogous universe, has collected multiple breeds of abandoned and injured pooches and other critters.

She currently has three dogs, two turtles and a dove. "That's the lowest census since I came to Marin County," she tells me. At one time, though unplanned, she had five canines. "I always think I'll find a home for them, but then I keep them. A friend who did dog-grooming realized I was a sucker."

I ask why she has no won't-power. "Once you have them and they trust you, it's hard to give them away. They'd have to start all over if you did."

Her preference is apparent: seniors. "Everyone wants puppies, so it's harder to place older dogs, especially those with problems." Aging canines enjoy years and years of domesticity with Patrice (one German Shepherd held on until 19). "They'll live a long time if they don't have stress in their lives," she explains.

Like human beings, I think.

Over the decades, she's invited a Setter, a Collie, a Tshi Tsu, a Schnauzer, and various mutts to co-habit with her, nurturing and nursing them until they die. Eleven are buried in her back yard, along with a 21-pound cat, Velcro, who'd been feral "but once he came inside never wanted to go out again."

One dog, she recalls impishly, was adopted "right after I had surgery. I was still under the influence of anesthesia."

Patrice never thinks of what she does as rescuing. "I just develop relationships with animals that people can't take care of," she says.

On rare occasion, more than one relationship will start concurrently: A poodle from the Marin Humane Society ("that came from a puppy mill that was shut down") was added to the Hickox home along with a beagle from the University of California at Davis ("that they'd originally planned to use in experiments as a research dog").

My friend's compassion touches me — especially when I think about her home menagerie.

In addition to dogs, cats, turtles, and doves, she's looked after a Conure parrot, two Amazon parrots and a Cockatiel. The birds all "had been dumped" at the WildCare rescue service while she volunteered there, doing hot line and other work for 10 years. "I thought I could make a difference," she says.

Patrice's love for other species dates to childhood, when she noticed her parents "were animal people — my father owned race-horses and my mother used to breed dogs."

Today she embraces numerous environmental issues as well as animal causes. A rebel without a pause, she is particularly bothered by "the use of pesticides in the wetlands

— I've seen them kill otters." She also loathes animal traps. Those negatives are offset, however, by the good feelings she gets walking "my decrepit dogs in [a park] where there are no cars, or around my neighborhood...and down by the creek."

Not far away, "dog fanatic" Joan Isaksen is another a pushover for needy canines. She's fostered 14.

And she works closely with Hopalong & Second Chance Animal Rescue, a nonprofit that merged two agencies in 2006 "in hopes of eliminating the euthanasia" of adoptable dogs and cats.

Joan volunteers in its office as adoption coordinator. But on a personal basis, fostering doesn't work out anymore. She presently houses three dogs — an Irish Wolfhound, a Shepherd mix, and a tiny Maltese — that were meant to be fosters but somehow turned into permanent guests. "I've been forbidden by my husband and son from bringing any more home," she informs me.

I'm not sure I buy it. I'd give odds the ban remains only until another homeless or stray pooch whimpers in front of her.

Joan's parents live only a block away. Because she works for a consulting firm in San Francisco, they help out by walking the dogs daily. "Rain or shine, we're out there," her dad, Heinz Feldman, says.

Joan, however, will always be the biped they cling to. "We try to give them boundaries, but a lot of dogs have slept on our bed," she admits. "I tell everybody they should train their dogs, but I'm a complete hypocrite: My dogs don't listen to me at all. They even follow me into the bathroom."

Her pets, she adds, "love my husband and love my son, but I'm definitely the alpha dog — and the big sucker, and they know it."

Sucker? I'm sure I've heard *that* dog-loving rationalization before. I've even used it myself. My wife and I, in fact, have rescued three Golden Retrievers. Our desire to sacrifice doesn't throb quite as energetically as Patrice's and Joan's, however, so we've done it serially — one pooch at a time.

Hairstylist to the stars now honing his acting chops

Inside his salon, Mitch Field flaunts two huge signs — Beauty and Sexy — and an oversized high school photo of Elvis. He readily admits to being a big fan of all three.

Mitch, thrice married, is an unabashed ladies' man enjoying a bachelor's life. Including the freedom to ogle. But "the first thing I see," he tells me, "is their hair, like a dentist seeing your teeth first."

The 68-year-old has been styling and studying hair since age 16 — though he started two years before, as "shampoo boy" for the legendary Vidal Sassoon, whose London salon was "the epicenter of modern hair design."

He became a Sassoon apprentice, he admits, because "it seemed like a good place to meet girls." I remember working in a New York bowling alley, also at 14, for the same reason.

Nowadays, Mitch limits appointments to three days a week. That gives him time to pursue a second career: acting. Which he's been perfecting for 12 years. And that doesn't count being in the "Woodstock" movie for a few seconds on a split screen with rocker Joe Cocker (my friend who'd come to the U.S. for San Francisco's Summer of Love had found a backstage pass in the mud that let him mingle with the concert's stars).

His later interest in theater stemmed from yet another penchant — hiking. Immersion happened rapidly: "I was leading a hike in 2004 and we went through the amphitheater on Mt. Tam and somebody said, 'The Mountain Play is going to do *My Fair Lady*. You should audition.' So, I did, and I got a role.

"While I was doing that show, [the guy] who was playing Henry Higgins said, 'I'm directing a show and you should audition.' So, I did, and I got it. It was *The Foreigner*. And while I was doing that, [another fellow] said, 'I'm directing a play and you should audition' — *45 Seconds from Broadway*, a Neil Simon comedy. I got that, too." Shortly thereafter, a third guy "was directing at the Marin Shakespeare Company and wanted me to go to work in *Two Gentlemen of Verona*. I also did *Romeo and Juliet* there that summer."

Mitch subsequently auditioned at the Berkeley Repertory Theatre, where he understudied half a dozen shows, including the current *Treasure Island*, in which he performs a number of roles. He's also done voice-overs, commercials, and independent films. And he's conducted 100 radio interviews, mostly with arts and entertainment folks, for *The Field Trip*, his Radio Sausalito series.

Unwilling to rest on any laurels, however, he looks ahead — "to bigger and better roles," and creating a tragicomic one-man show based on the life and heroin-related death of Free blues-rock guitarist Paul Kossoff.

Mitch hasn't minded taking a long time to get top billing. He's building theatrical memories that will match hairstyling reminiscences he rattles off as a raconteur.

He recalls, for instance, "a fun time in the '60s. London was swinging — with the Beatles, the Stones, Twiggy, fashion, mod, contraception…" And he recollects styling famed musicians Alice Cooper, Billy Idol, Adam Ant, and Eric Clapton in his Los Angeles salons. Not to mention Michael Richards, *Seinfeld* physical comic, with his trademark "do."

Why'd Mitch leave La-La-Land, where he spent a dozen years? "In L.A, you can be any of three things — young, good-looking, or both. Nothing else counts."

Mitch preferred morphing into scissors-and-comb artiste, fortified with more hair-colorings on his Fairfax salon's shelves than Michelangelo had hues on his palette. He now sports white hair and eyeglasses with frames of assorted colors ("You don't want to wear glasses that clash with your clothing if you can avoid it").

He favors dark dress pants, white shirt, and tie, rejecting current hairdresser picks — "flip-flops, cut-off shorts, white T-shirt, tattoos and piercing."

Mitch, who also called Montreal home for another 12 years, is particularly proud of his "personal service, including pre-styling consults with clients, and doing the whole job myself. No assistants." He does, however, occasionally work on two heads at a clip.

He doesn't want for much.

Spotting a sign recently that proclaims, 'When I grow up, I'm gonna do something else," makes me visualize him. But when I ask what he aspires to be on stage, the 5'7" charmer answers with a lone word: "Taller."

He's gone from coloring book to colorful views of candidates

Politics first beguiled Michael Rosenthal at age 5.

Rosey explains: When presented with "a coloring book of the presidents, I memorized them, their vice presidents, and their wives' names — and my parents trotted me out at parties to recite them."

He also remembers wrestling his best friend "in the way-back of a station wagon in 1960 with him yelling 'Nixon' and me yelling 'Kennedy.'"

Fast forward to today. My 61-year-old chum's hairline may have receded, but his progressive leanings haven't. "The choice between Hillary and Donald is so stark," he tells me. "It's disheartening to think that Trump even has a chance to become president…"

The voice of the University of California at Santa Cruz alum trails off into what I call The Thinking Zone, a place he visits often. But he's happy to share his musings, his bottomless research, and his colorful views of candidates and issues. In fact, he's been distributing his endorsements regularly since 1980, when he published his initial *Progressive Election Alert.*

"It was pretty crude at first," he recalls. "I'd type it out and insert oddly proportioned Xerox pictures. As computer technology improved, it started to look better."

Some 600 individuals now receive Rosey's email (as opposed to the postcard format he started with) about where "to send money to House and Senate races around the country," and how to vote on California ballot measures (17 of them this year).

But it's harder nowadays, he tells me. "A lot of these measures, I look at them and have to figure out what's the right thing to do. Some are purposely intended to fool you, like an evil twin, to keep you from voting for a good proposition."

Politics remains an avocation, though.

Career-wise, Rosey, a three-time Emmy-winning producer/editor, has worked for television magazine shows nationally and locally, on a feature film ("Never Cry Wolf"), and on multiple documentaries.

His favorite time period? *Bay Area Backroads*, from 1993 to 2008: "It was a dream job. I got paid to go out to interesting places and meet interesting people and tell stories about them." The KRON-TV series also helped him "cultivate a wonderful group of friends, people who are inspiring to be around."

He's back at the station once again, working "in part on *The BackStory*, a behind-the-scenes weekly look at how the news is gathered."

His favorite stomping ground, however, is his home in Fairfax (converted from a train station) and nearby open spaces.

Rosey's thoughtfulness merges with a glittery sense of humor. He refers to his dog, for example, as "five-and-a-half going on two." And he reminds me of an Artists for Social Responsibility parody poster he posed for years ago, "with my eyes crossed and a Jewish star." It satirized a faddish guru, Atmananda, "and a pretentious ad about past lives."

But he doesn't have to remind me of his 2003 wedding to Marleen Roggow only hours after "we sat inside a giant wedding ring in our float in the annual Fairfax Day Parade and the wedding party sang 'Going to the Chapel.'"

Nancy Fox, my wife, and I strolled in front. She wore a furry, life-sized costume and carried a huge cardboard ring. Voila! Ring bear-er. And I'd dressed in her nightgown and carried a wilted bouquet of daisies plucked from our back yard. Voila! Flower girl (with beard).

Rosey fondly remembers our silliness as well — as unmistakably as he remembers being impressed by Hillary quite some time ago. In 1986, actually. "At a conference in Little Rock, at a reception in the governor's mansion, when she was the state's First Lady, I talked to her and found her to be very smart, very compassionate." Rosey may not label her a perfect candidate (he'd "felt the Bern" in California's primary), but he surely detests the alternative.

A couple of weeks ago he was forced to change his website because his longstanding *url* had been hacked. Anyone who went there got what Marleen told me was "a scary warning about malware."

Neither he nor she, however, believes Russia was responsible. Or that anything's rigged. But they aren't willing to swear Donald didn't do it.

Sportscaster turns his surfing into waves of therapy

I'm a dinosaur.

At 79, I accept that my drying-out skin and print journalism — my lifelong profession — are both on the extinction trail of pterodactyls.

But I'm not quite ready to fade away. And although print may be following eight-tracks, horses-and-buggies, and dodos, I still prefer writing columns and texts *without* abbreviations, and I enjoy hearing local radio personalities rather than syndicated broadcasts.

OMG, how quaint!

Bruce Macgowan, 15 years my junior, doesn't fit the dino designation. Yet. But his journalistic playground — radio sportscasting — is also vanishing. That's listeners' loss: He's a good reporter. And a charming storyteller.

My Fairfax buddy has lately been successfully freelancing, seeking a new regular gig, and house-husbanding while his wife, Colette, teaches in a local Special Ed Department.

Bruce was born in San Francisco, a large baby: 10 pounds, 12 ounces, with long arms and legs. He morphed into a large man: 6 foot 6, and 220 pounds. His sports appetite is large, too — a hunger he's fed forever.

We're in an area restaurant when he recalls growing up in Marin County and knowing at 13 "I wanted to be a sportswriter or sportscaster." He actualized the fantasy.

"I've covered about 5,000 major sports events in my life," he tells me, "and I never get bored." He elaborates: "I like getting paid to watch what I enjoy. Part of the deal is being a fan. I think if you're not, you'd be miserable being in a ballpark 81 times a year."

Sports, Bruce contends, "are a metaphor for life, synthesizing the highs and lows, with moments of great drama and comedy."

He's completing his 41st year in broadcasting, but it hasn't been all fun and games. He admits he's "had anxiety issues since I was a kid, but I found that exercise mitigated them." That's why he surfs. "It's great exercise and a wonderful release. You're out in nature and it quiets the mind, soothes the spirit, and calms the body. It's my therapy."

On average, he surfs two or three times a week. He's so immersed that his Facebook profile photo features a breaking wave.

Part of Bruce's disquiet stems from haunting memories of his older brother, Paul, overdosing at age 36. He's also struggling with Colette's breast cancer. "She's living her life, day to day, to the fullest, doing everything possible to stay healthy, and doing everything she can to take care of the people she loves." But the illness worries him.

"I have good days and bad days, but it's a good lesson in how human beings can deal with adversity. I figure if she can handle it, I can too."

I notice that Bruce's casual attire somehow makes him look like he *is* handling it: Jeans, sandals, baseball cap, sunglasses dangling from the open neckline of a flannel shirt. For years, he'd worn a beard. Not today. Change time.

Not all changes are good, though, like what's happening in his field. Stations are using fewer local broadcasters. "I've been fired five times," Bruce reports without animosity.

But he's shocked by today's young broadcasters. "It's alarming. The kids' diction is bad, their vocabulary — and pronunciation — is amateurish."

Sports fans admire Bruce's professionalism, which comes from 17 years' experience at one station, KNBR, and stints at others in San Francisco, Eureka, Seattle, and Portland, plus UPI radio in New York. Add to that freelancing for stations in D.C. and New York as well as AP and NBC radio, not to mention CBC radio in Canada. He's also written columns for three Bay Area daily newspapers.

His most memorable coverage? "When the 1989 Giants baseball team won their first pennant in 27 years only to have the earthquake disrupt the World Series game at Candlestick [Park in San Francisco]."

When a buddy dies, it's time to mourn — and to change

David Brewer, a cherished friend for two decades and a surrogate brother for the one I never had, died a few days ago.

I'm fragile. In deep mourning. And reevaluating my life and priorities.

David's passing didn't come as a shock. He'd been battling a melanoma for years and the resultant metastasis for months. But death — despite my belief that the soul, or spirit, transcends it — feels so damned final. The empty hole it leaves can seem infinite.

It's likely you have a friend like David.

On his deathbed, my psychologist/consultant pal, still boyishly good-looking despite being sixty-something, and still a pigheaded St. Louis Cardinals fanatic, revisited his spiritual feelings. He re-told me of his "awakening" at 19, when he'd deduced that spirit was an embodiment "of compassionate love" rather than the anthropomorphic being others worshipped.

Though he'd been brought up an ardent Christian and I'd been reared as a Jew, we'd found a joint comfort zone. I miss him. But I consider myself lucky — blessed, in fact — to have had him in my life so long. As a loving, trusted friend. As a colleague in a men's group for 10 years. As a dog sitter in my home.

I have fond memories, too, of others who'd been essential parts of my life but, in Hamlet's words, have shuffled off this mortal coil. And there are many: My parents and grandparents, a woman I lived with in Philadelphia, two first cousins who died in their teens. All told, death in double digits — more than sufficient for any lifetime.

But David's death has shifted my perspective.

No longer am I irked by the almost constant road construction near my home. Or the dog poop I barely miss while walking our purebred mutt downtown. Or the incredibly long wait at traffic lights at the hub that should probably be turned into a roundabout. Instead, I linger longer to watch two newborn fawns in my yard, to catch the wonderment of a sunset from our deck, to see toddlers frolic in a playground.

My friends, wife, kids, and grandkids unsurprisingly have leapt anew to the top of my what's-important list. I vow to phone and email more yet retain my right to *not* text.

I choose to elevate my sensitivity at Marin Man to Man, a weekly support group I run that's aimed at helping guys whose partners have breast cancer or another life-threatening disease. And to spend added hours with the 11 friends facing severe health challenges. I intend, too, to fully appreciate that I'm comparatively healthy — still breathing and able to pound my keyboard long enough to cobble columns together.

Did David's death, or life, mean more than any of the 8,000 killed in Nepal's late April quake? He and I'd often pondered that kind of question, always concluding life anywhere was equal to either of our own.

I'll remember him as an imperfect perfectionist who left behind a lengthy string of wives, girlfriends, and broken hearts, but moreover that he was himself even in his last moments exuding life and love.

Shortly before being hospitalized, my buddy, the quintessential organizer — he was forever arranging a last-second movie group or dinner klatch or something-else cluster — had corralled a small group of friends. In a sense, it was his last hurrah. He knew the prognosis.

My 8-year-old granddaughter traipsed along. David, childless, had attached himself to her years before but decided on the spot that day she'd be his "date" for the party. So, he showered her with attention, including the hugs for which he was famous, and bought her a huge cookie.

Too soon afterward he proved that death *can* incorporate dignity. And courage. And joking.

He and I and my wife reminisced and laughed multiple times during our final conversation. I doubt if he'd primped for our appearance, but he reportedly did for at least two women who followed us individually.

In tribute to his tangible influence on my life, I hope to assuage my sadness with an amped up zest for living and doing. And to continue fighting for the environment, for the homeless, for equal rights.

I'm sure David would approve.

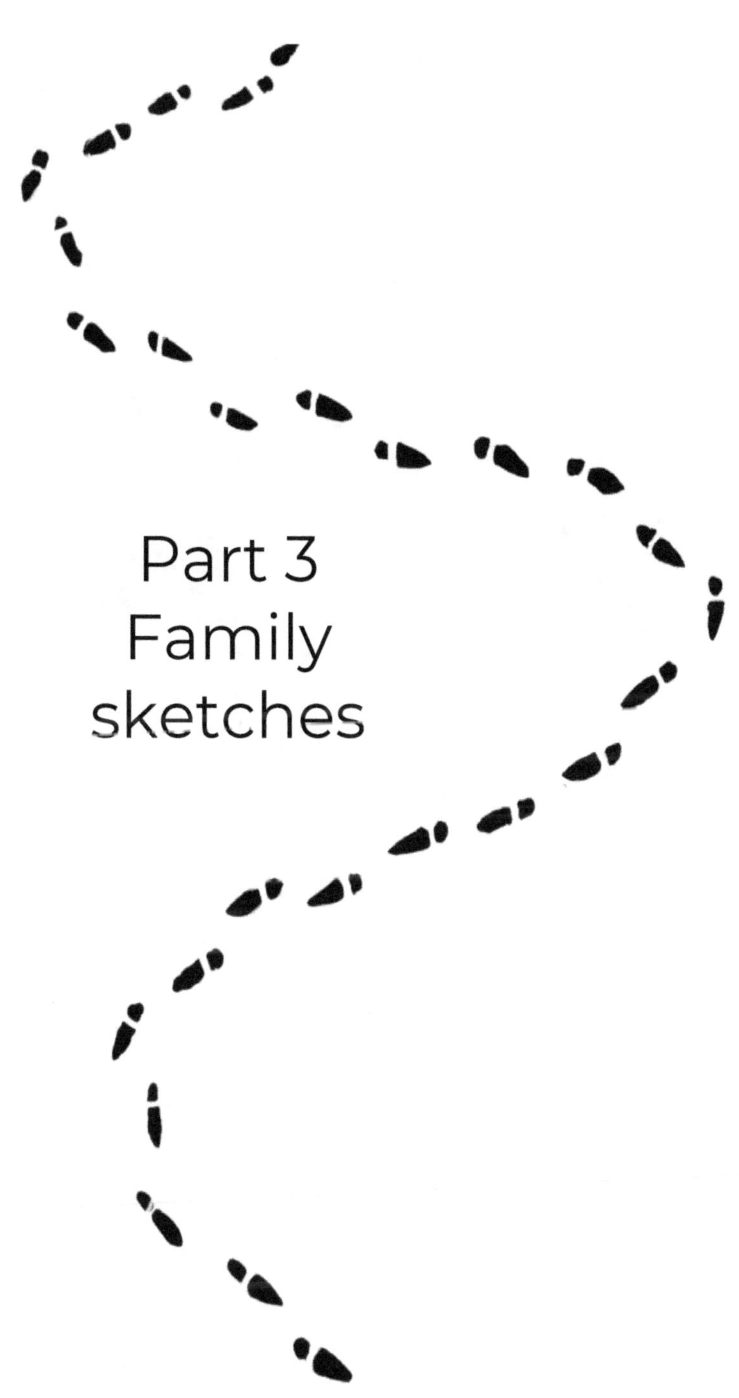

Part 3 Family sketches

She's playful, opinionated, cautious, loving – and four

It was so hot my granddaughter guzzled the huge lemonade through four straws at once — two of hers, one of mine, one of my wife's.

Though Hannah Schifrin normally shares, the heat made her me-ness grow exponentially and her mouth slurp almost as fast as the final space shuttle would zoom off a few days later.

We were enjoying the Marin County Fair, where the temp would have passed 93 in the shade had there been any.

I was positive my deodorant wouldn't hold.

My wife and I have enjoyed the event often but never before experienced it through the wide-eyed perspective of a four-year-old. It's way more fun that way, better even than our previously hearing a library concert with her, seeing a talented kids' performer, or trial-and-erroring at the science-based Exploratorium or Discovery Museum.

We started with the petting zoo, where Hannah flitted from animal to animal in a blur, her short attention span locked into top gear.

She waddled like a duck and clucked like a chicken one second, squatted near and stared at a llama the next. In successive flashes, she became infatuated with a donkey and a hog. Micro-moments later, she exclaimed, "Oh, look, there's a mommy goat, and there are her babies!"

But when I asked if she wanted to stroke an infant kangaroo, she knowingly corrected me: "You're silly — that's a wallaby."

Close by was a large pen containing four tiny three-month-old piglets. "They're cute," conceded Hannah. "The white one looks like Wilbur, a piggy from *Charlotte's Web*. I have both the video and the book."

I don't know if she learned from an app on her iPad, but a biology lesson from our preschooler followed. "Oh, grandpa, look, that's the biggest milk cow I've ever seen. The udders are on the back side. I can see them from here. Those dairy goats have udders, too. That's the mommy. I can tell because she's big."

Because the heat drenched us, we paused in the barn, sitting on bales and ignoring how much hay stuck to our clothes.

On to Golden Gate Pavilion, blessedly air-conditioned, filled with exhibit after exhibit commemorating the 75th birthday of the bridge. Hannah strolled across a 48-foot-long replica, then watched ping-pong balls wiggle through a sculpture Scott Weaver had built from 100,000 toothpicks. "That was cool," she decided.

Her amusement didn't last.

As we checked out rows and rows of paintings on display, she became resolute: "I want to be someplace else."

We therefore couldn't scrutinize two local ribbon-winners we'd stumbled on, and we had to skip "Sunrise on Fern Hill" by Dan Thomas, our next-door neighbor who spent part of his fair time singing in a barbershop quartet, part tooling around with *his* grandchild, two-year-old Desmond.

Suddenly, Princess Leia of *Star Wars* floated by, trailed by a self-propelled version of R2-D2. She was soundless; the robot, however, rattled and squeaked. Hannah, who'd been scared two years ago by a deafening horn at a parade, clutched at my waist and pants leg.

We scurried outside, my granddaughter piloting ("I want to be the leader"). She spied the Giant Ferris Wheel in the distance, and her misgivings amplified. "I don't want to go on that," she proclaimed. "I went on one somewhere else and throwed up and didn't feel so good."

Our smartest move was to say nothing.

The same held true when, as we meandered through the ride-and-game midway, I heard a disgruntled mother say, "He didn't want to do the things that are free, but he wanted to throw darts at $5 a pop and spend $100 for a $2 toy."

Hannah soon shrugged off any bad feelings and was tugging my wife's hand — toward a booth with balloons featuring images of her favorite characters, Dora the Explorer and Diego, Dora's sidekick.

Even though we know our main job these days is to spoil the grandchild, we didn't buy any. We directed her instead to the pig races. Hannah squealed gleefully, louder than the porkers. But the announcer's voice was so thunderous she covered her ears. She therefore didn't hear when he told a groan-inducing tale of a losing piggy who'd pulled a hamstring.

We left satisfied, part of the 117,000 who attended Marin's 66th annual fair and paid record admissions of $1.3 million.

We'd been particularly happy watching Hannah be particularly happy. But my best moment came when, without coaching, she'd stretched her arms wide and shouted, "Grandpa, I love you *that* much."

Yeah, I love that.

And I love that my heat rash has faded.

However, although it's been weeks now, I'm still picking up strands of hay from the seats and floor of my car.

My little girl turns 50, with unforeseen touches of high drama

I wished for an instant I was curled up in fetal position, sucking my thumb, in bed at home in Northern California.

Instead, I was in Yonkers, a New York City suburb, watching my wife, Nancy Fox, play a concert-grand Steinway piano to a nearly empty 300-seat library auditorium following a complete publicity screw-up by the staff.

And that misadventure followed a 9-1-1 call to help my daughter, Jan Brown, who'd had a diabetic meltdown in a fancy-schmancy deli.

Not quite the 50th birthday celebration for her we'd envisioned.

Toward the rear of the auditorium sat an unidentified elderly couple that physically reminded me of Fred and Ethel Mertz from *I Love Lucy*. My daughter, son, grandson, and I scattered around the room, pretending we were part of a mob scene. "Looks like I'm playing for my family, two new friends and 294 ghosts," said my wife, a pro.

"I was scheduled to play Oscar-winning songs," Nancy announced, "but if any of you have requests, I'll play them instead — *after* I start with the first Academy Award tune, 'The Continental,' which has special meeting for me: It was my parents' song. It was playing the night they met, the same night my father proposed."

Vigorous applause — exceedingly robust considering there were only six of us — greeted her finish.

Jan asked for "Sunrise, Sunset," a mega-sentimental tune from *Fiddler on the Roof*, and the couple we didn't know followed with requests for Cole Porter songs: "Begin the Beguine" and "Let's Do It." Nancy cheerfully played them and two dozen more.

Six people swayed to her hour-long artistry. The ghosts? Well, I couldn't hear their applause, but I'm positive they gave her a standing ovation, too.

My wife had planned the concert as a surprise gift, intending to dedicate it to Jan. But my disabled daughter had been so excited to see us she'd forgotten to eat breakfast — and then taken her insulin anyway. Blood sugar tailspin! The paramedics helped her recover just in time for me to whisk her to the auditorium.

Regrettably, a similar incident occurred days later.

Jan's top birthday wish? No diamonds. No caviar. Just paper that wouldn't stop up her apartment's toilet like the brand she'd been using. So, I drove her to Costco. But Jan's blood sugar decided to react badly to meds she'd taken. Nosedive No. 2!

My daughter eventually got her wish, but the purchase jerked me back to a happier moment in a supermarket in San Anselmo, where I reside.

A day after I'd interviewed Ram Dass, we ran across him in an aisle there buying odds and ends. Nancy giggled. "What's funny?" I asked. "Well," she said, pointing to the toilet paper the world-renowned thinker had stuffed under his arm, "that's the great cosmic equalizer, isn't it?" All three of us chuckled.

Being able to give life and its pitfalls a horselaugh, I'm convinced, is definitely the best medicine.

Heading back home, Nancy and I sailed through airport security. While putting my belt back on, however, it broke. Using one hand to pull my carry-on, the other to keep my pants from dropping to my knees, I entered every shop that might peddle belts. None stocked anything to fit my size-43 waist. So, Nancy and I did what we could: We cackled. I bought one later, at the other end.

In the meantime, however, I had time to ponder a pair of positive anecdotes Jan had recalled: "I remember listening — as a child lying on a couch in your den — to the tick-tick-tick of your typewriter and staring at the thousands of books that went up to the ceiling," she'd said. "And I remember another time, having the school call home to ask where I was. I was methodically chipping away at ice because there was a dollar frozen in it."

Her memories moved me.

Being a dad can be tough in the best of times. Being the father of a disabled person can be especially difficult, particularly when she lives 2,560 air miles away. But I have no plans to trade her in. Jan is bright, sensitive, and generous with her love and time and money — a caring mom and daughter.

My trip was emotionally draining, mentally draining, physically draining. But worth it. After all, she'll always be my little girl. Besides, I was able to bask in her good feelings when I bought her some new clothes and a dresser to keep them in.

As her great-grandma used to beseech God, "Let her use them in good health."

My son's hip surgery thrusts me into a tricky role

My live-alone son's accident yanked me out of my comfort zone.

Suddenly I found myself jetting to Atlanta, squeezed in an emotional vise between the pangs of separation from my wife and the trickiness of caregiving for an adult child.

During a 27-year tenure in San Anselmo, I've never been absent for a month. Nor have I ever been away from my wife, Nancy, that long. But Mark's workplace fall meant he needed an instant hip replacement — and help. So, I wasted no time getting there, even though I knew I'd be walking a thin line between usefulness and intrusion.

The visit wasn't without lighter moments.

Like when an old vacuum cleaner being donated to Goodwill rolled into the street because I hadn't noticed his driveway's incline.

Or when I became ecstatic cooking for the first time in years because I didn't burn the water.

Or when I found it imperative to bop to the supermarket virtually every day because I'd forgotten one item or another.

Spoiler alert: My independent 48-year-old six-footer's recovery is coming along just fine, thank you. He graduated from his hospital bed to a wheelchair to a walker to a cane. He abandoned his knee-high support hose and brace. He even had a haircut and shaved off his stubble.

I, meanwhile, got so jammed being an imposter nurse/wife/janitor in Georgia that I knew zilch about reports that the American Psychiatric Association declared taking selfies to be a form of mental illness, David Letterman retiring, or Russia and Ukraine and Crimea playing last country standing.

Similar to the wolf in *The Three Little Pigs*, I huffed and puffed (appropriate to my senior status). Instead of blowing my son's house down, however, I cleaned it up (appropriate to my being a neatnik and a cleanliness freak).

And — hooray! — I lost six pounds in the process.

But my first day there I also lost three full hours driving around looking for non-existent signage and stopping at fast-food joints only to get faulty advice from well-intentioned but direction-clueless southerners.

Mark was mildly anxious I'd depict him as an invalid. He needn't have worried: I view him as anything but. He was courageous throughout, bulldozing past his vulnerability, speeding his healing by completing more exercises than his physical therapist ordered. And he made sure to do — without help from me, his 17-year-old son Zach, or a part-time healthcare worker — whatever he could.

Despite his pain, rarely did he become cranky (though he loathed not being able to go back to work immediately).

My spirits often needed more bolstering than his. So, Nancy rang twice a day to inject verbal booster shots. Her calls were inevitably packed with love, except for the evening I cited flirting with a young nurse in the surgeon's office. She didn't find that amusing at all. My male friends — well-wishers via cell and computer — were more empathetic.

Edible assistance was never far away.

Hannah, my granddaughter, sent via UPS delectable cookies she'd made from scratch alongside Nancy.

Patrice, Mark's ex-wife, provided foodstuffs, too — enough to satiate a battalion: lasagna, brisket, spaghetti, meatloaf, plus copious salads.

Also among our most valuable gifts were tips from Anya Schandler, an angel/friend who'd undergone hip replacement surgery a short time before. Mark and I had abundant time to discuss — and implement — them. And to scrutinize many other things: My newfound love for the dollar store. The junk that filled his garage. The intensity of *Breaking Bad* (we binge-watched three seasons' worth). A leaky roof. Recycling 1,100 plastic bags. And my inability, as a Mac user, to work his PC without about 25 typing errors per line.

Flying home, too exhausted to sleep, I listened to an hour-long NPR program about turning mistakes into opportunities. I contemplated my typos — and Mark's fall.

Once back, I returned to my again-insatiable addiction: a daily 90-minute morning diet of online news. And to mulling the dry, dry Marin County climate. Nancy had started an "if it's yellow, let it mellow" toilet protocol. I agreed to follow her lead. Just like in the last drought.

She remarked, too, that she'd spotted a rainbow just as I was coming home. We agreed it was a sign of something good.

No more accidents, hopefully.

Robin Williams becomes the icing on family-vacation cake

And the winner is — drumroll, please — comedian/actor Robin Williams.

Three generations of my family unanimously agreed his improv at a local theater immediately became the apex of a recent San Francisco Bay Area vacation. The icing on our cake, you might say.

He headlined a bill that included funnyman Mort Sahl, who at 85 walks haltingly but retains a keen mind.

I'd actually planned for our East Coast visitors to catch a weekly Mark Pitta & Friends gag-filled gig, so was surprised to find us watching 90 minutes of improvisation as beneficiaries of a scheduling switch. *Set List,* "stand-up without a net," was being filmed for United Kingdom telecasting.

Each comic was captivating but Robin, undoubtedly his generation's primo comedy genius, exceeded everyone's expectations. His steel-trap mind was fully transparent.

He instantly absorbed the never-before-seen phrases that flashed on a screen behind him, weaving them into a web of delight. And yes, much of his humor wasn't for little kids — especially his uproarious rendition of a talking vagina.

But my 15-year-old grandson guffawed. So did my other grandson, who's 24; my son, 46; and my wife, who's been on the planet only two years less than my 74 years. She, in fact, noted that "Sahl was as sharp as a tack and Williams as sharp as two tacks."

I shared her evaluation and the entire family's euphoria.

I'd been in the 128 Throckmorton theater in Mill Valley many times, mostly to hear readings of plays by a group with a self-describing moniker, Writers with Attitude. But I know that the remodeled nonprofit, which dates back to 1915 when it showed Charlie Chaplin flicks for a few pennies, has also been the site of concerts and jam sessions that include the likes of Joan Baez and Woody Allen (individually, not as a duet).

While planning the vacation for "the boys," I momentarily thought I had 7,150,739 places to choose from — one each Bay Area resident counted in the census might recommend. At least that's what it felt like when I invited suggestions from friends and colleagues.

The ideas poured in.

One of the best recommendations was the San Francisco Movie Tour, a three-hour bus ride featuring 70 clips from 60 films shot in the city. Wylie Herman, an actor well versed in cinematic lore, guided us. Humor and Hollywood back-lot scraps copiously trickled off his tongue.

When discussing the filming of a Mike Myers' comedy, *So I Married an Axe Murderer*, for instance, he cited a Tinsel Town aphorism feared by actors and adored by Realtors: "The camera adds 10 pounds and five bedrooms."

Another of my family's faves was a visit to the California Academy of Sciences, which was featuring a new exhibit and planetarium show, *Earthquake*. A couple of dubious moments resurfaced for my spouse and me, however, because we'd been downtown when the Loma Prieta tremor hit in 1989.

The boys appreciated it more. They also enjoyed the permanent displays — the waddling penguins and always-exhilarating underwater creatures of the Steinhart Aquarium. But all of us expressly reveled in the ostrich chicks, then 16 days old.

Alcatraz, of course, is consistently on or near the top of tourist must-lists. It was no exception for us. A walking tour of the site last used as a prison in 1963 was jammed with facts, facts, and more facts, including solar panels having been recently installed to generate 80 percent of the needed power.

My wife was staggered, though, to find "prisoners had been segregated. I'd never thought about that before."

Next up was The Magic Bus, a two-hour multimedia "time machine" tour of San Francisco that recreates the Summer of Love and the city's Haight-Ashbury heyday. Music from the "sex, drugs and rock 'n' roll" decade blasted through the bus as retractable screens depicted scene after scene of local happenings, interviews about acid trips and psychedelics, and a historical context. They transformed each of us into a Dr. Feelgood.

We also got off wearing 3-D glasses that made the bus wallpaper and souvenir booklet photos jump out.

But I teared up again when the assassinations of John and Bobby Kennedy, Martin Luther King flashed before my eyes and brain.

My wife and I, who'd both done the '60s consciously rather than being in an illegal-substance fog, liked the bubble-discharging ride better than my kin, one of whom had been a toddler and two who hadn't even been conceived. Our pleasure was even enhanced by bumper-sticker wisdom offered by the hippie-clad tour guide: "Life is to be lived, not just tolerated."

Living it to the fullest, for us, meant additional stops at Pier 39, where we all marveled in the Mirror Maze (one of the seemingly endless tourist attractions and views, restaurants, and shopping opportunities there), and the Conservatory of Flowers, where we saw *Plantosaurus Rex*, an exhibit of "living fossils" (prehistoric plants), along with models of dinosaurs (with one sticking its head through the roof).

When all was said and done, though, the biggest vacation takeaway for me was the discovery that the boys walked too fast for my spouse/partner and me to keep pace. I guess it's appropriate that the Summer Olympics are in full swing: We definitely need to pass the foot-race torch.

I celebrate my dog's life – and simultaneously taste mortality

My wife and I watched a vet put Halley into a perma-sleep last month.

Our "Golden oldie," a rescued Retriever, had lived till almost 16 — somewhere around 110 in people years. But that didn't feel nearly long enough for us. On some level I'd hoped she'd become a doggie version of Methuselah. Or Lazarus.

No such luck.

Zillions undoubtedly have experienced similar emotions when their pet dogs, cats, llamas or you-name-its died.

One of my fleeting sensations was misplaced anger, which strong-armed me into snapping at my no-less fragile wife several days after the euthanasia. But she understood my rawness and immediately forgave me.

Together, she and I had rubbed Halley's snow-white snout and ultra-soft fur for the last time in a tiny room at an emergency pet center. Though death came peacefully, it set off an avalanche of tears. Which has yet to stop. The sudden hole in our lives and home still triggers erratic bursts of waterworks.

We did manage, however, to ponder a syrupy poem, "Rainbow Bridge," which sketches a pre-heaven site where restored animals purportedly await their caregivers. And we jotted down five full pages of happy memories at a celebration-of-life lunch.

I fondly remembered Halley's tongue becoming a pre-rinse cycle for dinner plates when I'd open the dishwasher, and her licking the sweat off my body after my treadmill-and-recumbent bike exercises. I also radiated at the thought of my getting extra exercise picking up clumps of hair she'd shed. I recalled, too, hundreds of post-rainstorm walks in which she, like our young granddaughter, made certain she pounced into every muddy puddle.

Halley sure made us feel wonderful, though it didn't work in reverse: She never once giggled at my jokes.

My wife enjoyed memories of Halley constantly following her everywhere, even into the bathroom; thrusting her head into our laps as requests for petting; frolicking with other canines but preferring the company of homo sapiens; requiring her pills be wrapped in cheese before she'd swallow them; carrying frayed slippers to the front door so guests could inspect each stain; and trying to scratch holes into our carpeting so she might stash well-chewed rawhide bones.

We both loved watching her gotcha chase-games: tennis balls launched from a Chuckit, squirrels up trees, raccoons down drains, ducks and geese in waterholes. And, since she was hardly No. 1 in her dog-training class, skunks waddling up our potholed roadway.

We adored pee-and-poop walks with her at local parks and on endless trails in nearby hills. And we were amused by her laissez-faire, pro forma barking at a doe or hidden coyote out back, owls camouflaged in our oaks, wild turkeys that deigned to promenade on the deck, and even leaves rustling in the trees.

We reveled in our "old lady" being a chick magnet for me and a stud magnet for my spouse, though neither of us would ever dream of taking advantage of that advantage.

And we chuckled at her snoring being as loud and frequent as ours, not to mention her passing gas silently, so unobtrusively we couldn't tell if she or one of us were the guilty party.

We didn't perceive her as a pet but as a late-in-life child we'd adopted years after I and my wife had been "fixed" by surgeons.

Her happy spirit, like her fur, is everywhere. I turn often, in hopes of seeing her follow me up the stairs, greeting us at the door, or protecting my visiting granddaughter's bedroom from goblins.

Not surprisingly, Halley's death made me taste my own mortality. I flashed back, for instance, to a scene from two decades ago. My wife and I were flying in a Singapore Airlines jet that almost crashed into another plane on a Hong Kong runway. I instantly had to decide if I were OK with dying. Yes, I'd told myself, I'd lived "a good life, been a good person," and accomplished most of what I'd wished to do. So, I relaxed and let the captain and God, his co-pilot, take over.

I lived, of course, and didn't think about death again until I was forced to face my wife's breast cancer, her melanoma and my own prostate cancer. I got through all of those just a trifle worse for wear. I also survived the year I was convinced I was going to die, having had a series of scary premonitions.

As for now, I don't need no stinkin' pity parties. I plan to employ a soupçon of strained insouciance to work through the sadness. Besides, I'm hoping to luck out and stick around until I go quickly and peacefully at, well, somewhere near 110.

Just like Halley.

Part 4
Quickie insights

Humor, wisdom, pathos – all are within earshot

I'm an eavesdropper. Unintentionally, of course.

Like most folks, I can't help overhearing intriguing snatches of conversation from time to time, here and there. I'm frequently amused, and on rare occasions moved.

So, with apologies to Jimmy Cannon, Leah Garchik and all the daily newspaper columnists who've toyed with this sort of thing way before now, here are some morsels I've tuned in on recently near my home and elsewhere. All are accurate, give or take an edited word or two.

A perky blonde in tight shorts shopping in the men's department at Macy's whimpers to a gal-pal, "It's a shame, he doesn't speak jewelry."

Declares a tattooed twentyish man with spiked hair, studded leather jacket and combat boots to a second chap looking just as menacing on a main drag: "He's got the people skills of a petrified dog turd."

An unruly boy, who couldn't be more than five, orders his dad in a yogurt shop to "give me a treat or I'll breathe fire on you."

A straw-hatted woman in her late 60s, pearl choker reflecting the sun in a supermarket parking lot, complains,

"This morning I had to remove a hair from my chin that was so long I felt I had to give it a name."

While I laze on the Town Hall lawn before a meeting, I hear a chunky middle-aged female theorize this: "Lots of my busy friends tell me they've got too much on their plates. Could that be what's behind our country's obesity epidemic?"

An older blue-collar type in the local library chats with an aide: "I've got two puppies now — my latter-day children."

At Home Depot, a young fellow with baggy pants and long yellow locks streaked with blue explains to a buddy, "Put it together myself? You gotta be kidding. The most effort I want to put out is to write a check."

I catch a rosy-faced toddler outside the jumpy house at a fair saying to her grandmother, "I can't stop hugging you *because* I love you."

At a gathering of political activists in a private mansion, the prim hostess describes a wannabe office holder like this: "If her IQ dropped any lower, you'd have to water her twice a day."

This one makes me want to know more. A midlifer on her cell on yet another street corner: "You're in some kind of effin' mood today. I love you. Goodbye."

One bearded, dreadlocked guy talks to another on a street corner: "The cops broke up the Occupy Wall Street rally before there was any trouble whatsoever. I'd call that premature evacuation."

High schooler in a short skirt tells her boyfriend at a Subway restaurant, "He's a thundermouth."

A man on a bench wearing a wool cardigan: "My wife told me, 'I know it's not that cold outside, but inside my body, it's winter.

In a coffee shop, a raven-haired beauty sarcastically snaps at her younger male companion, "Don't worry your pretty little head about it."

At an outdoor concert near a creek, a multi-wrinkled woman notes, "They're playing my dermatologist's theme song, Cole Porter's 'I've Got You Under My Skin.'"

Younger man outside a nearby market says, "I take it for granted they'll always sell toilet paper and I'll never have to use leaves."

A teenage girl walking her dog at the local high school comments, "I swear I'm *not* superstitious, but I walk under no ladders, take no risks on Friday the 13th, and shudder if a black cat crosses my path."

Male with salt-and-pepper hair tugs at his ear while in the ticket line at a movie house and says, "I can't believe I have outlived my penis."

And one final thought: If anyone was in the bagelry the other day, they might have overheard me tell my wife, "Some people live like they're a quart of milk, but I prefer acting as if I have no expiration date."

I chew and chew on overheard chit-chat

No, of course I don't eavesdrop on purpose.

But I do unintentionally ingest conversational crumbs during my dog-walking stints or other local meanderings.

I've learned that my town and neighboring communities are veritable hotbeds of amusing or thought-provoking verbal tidbits. Such as the following, extracted from a pile of scribbled notes hither and yon on my desk:

Two girl bicyclists rest, cross-legged, on a downtown sidewalk. Says one, "When I first met my boyfriend, he was feral."

Laments a white-haired chap to a checker in a supermarket, "When I see how many of my gismos, thingamajigs and appliances are breaking down, some after only 30 or 40 days, I hate to think about what's going on in my body after 92 years."

Chatting outside a nearby residence, a redheaded midlifer tells a male companion, "I thought Hostess was defunct, but I was wrong. Twinkies and Ho-Hos have new outlets. Which confirms what I've always believed — they have a shelf-life that ensures they, along with the cockroaches, will inherit the Earth."

At a dog park behind another food outlet, a twenty-something guy rhetorically asks a chum, "Did you hear that canines here communicate via pee-mail?"

Husband in tattered shorts to loud wife in basic black outside the Post Office: "I heard what you meant."

A bluehair leaning on a cane at the gas station says to a driver, "I don't know about you, but I can never rest in a restroom."

Angry young woman to red-faced young man in a park: "I am *not* a stand-in in your movie."

As they both caress an assortment of nuts and bolts at a hardware store, a young man with a nose-ring tells his girlfriend, who has both eyebrows pierced, "He got his B.A. degree in B.S."

Succinctly, on the Town Hall lawn, a female teenager informs a gal pal, "I don't do boredom."

A fortyish guy on the campus of a nearby community college educates a younger classmate, "When anyone calls a celebrity 'a legend,' that means the person being referred to is old, old, old — or dead."

At a veterinary hospital, a mom asks her daughter: "When all the newspapers disappear, will puppies be trained on Kindles?"

Unsteady gray-haired guy in front of a wine bar who's clearly done more than taste: "My life can be measured in troublesome channels. When I was five, it was Guadalcanal. Now, it's my alimentary canal."

While discussing her daughter's new boyfriend, a stylish woman heading into a night club tells a companion, "My inner jury's still out."

Comments one smiling matron to another as they window-shop a variety store, "Having just learned that an American Headache Society exists gives me a headache."

Says one twinkle-eyed blonde in front of a third supermarket to another, "She's a magnet for desperadoes."

Repartee overheard at a bus stop: "Greeting cards are getting expensive." "Yeah, but now they talk, sing and do your laundry."

A redhead sips a latte in a coffee shop and gripes, after what she reports as her second date with the new man in her life, "I have yet to find his sense of humor or personality."

An acne-ridden teen boy, licking a spoon in front of a Gelato shop: "I believe in stating the obvious — because most people overlook it."

"I'm 87 years old and still very much a work in progress," says a woman to her companion in a Thai restaurant.

In the doorway of the bicycle repair shop, a youth whispers to himself, "She's somewhere between perfect and Oh, My God."

A housefrau enters a camera shop telling one friend about another: "He lives partly in Manhattan, partly in Florida, and wholly in yesterday."

A high school student describes a verbose acquaintance thusly: "He's a wordaholic."

And here's my personal favorite: A bald philosopher-king outside a hair salon says, "My recommendation for a bumper sticker is: 'Life is not a bumper sticker.'"

Selfie-ing, snooping, swearing – etc., etc., etc., and so forth

Messing up my desk — in addition to Post-its galore — are often-illegible scribbles on crumpled napkins and torn notepad pages.

Haphazard odds 'n' ends. Brainstorms worthy of repeating immediately, even if most of them are self-indulgent, first-person one- or two-liners. Or, perhaps, wannabe *bon mots* unworthy of being repeated to any living human being ever.

What follows are the former, I hope. Which should prove I still can tell the difference. So…

- There must be something terribly wrong with me: I've never taken a selfie.
- Yep, I may be a social misfit: I've never pierced any part of my body, subjected myself to tattooing, or even worn a hoodie.
- Although I've zero reasons to be paranoid, I still worry about governmental alphabet soup. Whenever I see a parked black van with no lettering on its sides and no windows, I envision a CIA, NSA or FBI agent crouched inside with state-of-the-art snooping equipment.

- A waggish friend asked me this: If a deaf child signs swear-words, should his mom wash out his hands with soap?
- No matter how often pals urge me *not* to be that way, I'm judgmental. I figure God gave me the capability and who are I to argue with Him (or, as my wife contends, Her)?
- I probably won't get my mojo back, at least until I figure out what that phrase really means.
- In spite of pundits swearing the U.S. economy has recovered, a downtown stroll reveals vacant stores, proving that retail is still hurting — and I'd bet local restaurants will be in even deeper doo-doo when Amazon perfects hot-meal deliveries by drone.
- My nine-year-old granddaughter made me a trinket that says, "Grandpa rocks." I love that view, even if she's mistaken.
- Words and phrases that I'm hesitant to slip into a column: kerfuffle, just sayin', hyper-hyperbolic, mythomaniac, peripheral hearing, tongue-in-chic.
- Some folks wear their emotions on their sleeves; some nouveau riche in this area wear their wallets on their sleeves.
- Whadda ya mean I'm talking in riddles? You must be listening in riddles.
- Janet Yellen and her Fed may believe inflation is moving unhurriedly but I think otherwise: The only thing you can get nowadays for a $10 bill is ten ones.
- A sleek, brown-and-white bobcat recently loped through our back yard. He/she/it was gorgeous. Hey, I wonder — maybe because it's suddenly trendy — if there's any such thing as a transgender cougar.

- Hooray! El Niño turned into greenery our yard's former brownery.
- I not long ago left a drama at intermission not because the play was bad but because my seat was totally unsittable (don't write to me: I know that word's not in most folks' lexicons).
- Too many oldsters I know aren't hard of hearing, they're hard of listening.
- Some artworks in my home have hung so long they're invisible — except when they get crooked, and my obsessive-compulsiveness demands I straighten them.
- Half a century after I escaped the area, I'm still a recovering New Yawker.
- *The Big Bang Theory* is still a major chortle-athon for me (despite its irritating laugh-track), but my wife avers it's downright unfunny (she claims it starts out slowly, then grinds to a dead-end).
- Will I ever be able to approach any cactus plant on my property without getting pricked?
- My handwriting has become as legible as that of a stoned centipede.
- Everything in my life is grist for the mill (or, more accurately, grist for this column — which sometimes bugs my wife, whom I apparently quote quite often when she's not looking).

Post-its help me vent, amuse, and flaunt my ignorance

I'm an itsy-bitsy old-fashioned: I'd rather use a Post-it than an iPhone's notepad.

So, I ring my iMac with instant reminders, to-do lists, and quick- or slow-witted brainstorms — as I've been doing forever.

The yellow stickies also sit on my desk in three piles (do-it-now, do-it-asap, and fergettaboudit!). And I usually have a pad in my pants pocket, just in case.

Though the mini-notes don't define either my universe or my homestead, they do let me prioritize what I think is fascinating or merely important. They also frequently offer pleasure or amusement. Such as a verbal bon-bon from my wife that I hereby reproduce here: "I'm counting my blessings — and you're a lot of them."

Then there's this, from a source I can't decipher, "Hyperventilation is proof we're still breathing."

Sometimes the notes are edgy. Such as, "Overheard geezer talking to a companion in the library, 'My wife accuses me of being a pochemuchka, which is a Russian word for someone who asks too many questions.'"

A friend bemoans the steady San Francisco Opera diet of Italian offerings: 'It's pasta, pasta, pasta all the time,' he complains."

In contrast, some Post-its merely give me a chance to vent:

• "Recent 5-4 right-wing rulings of the U.S. Supreme Court don't pass my personal stink test."

• "With tech support being what it is — outsourced and understaffed — I spend way too much time on hold with the Philippines and India."

Sometimes I question the so-called evolution of our society: "When did 'a learning experience' get replaced with 'a teaching moment'? And why?"

Or ponder what just happened: "Was standing in our back yard when a gray squirrel mistook me for a tree and ran up my pants leg, then my arm. I brushed it off, then trembled as, watching it scamper up a real trunk, I realized it might be rabid."

Because I'm so fond of word play, I've enjoyed glancing at this scrawl more than once, "Overheard, from moped-walking young woman in a parking lot — 'He makes so many mistakes, his life is a reign of error.'"

Perfect for a musician? "Nobody knows the treble I've seen."

More than a handful of sticky notes are personal: "Because I often write about my songwriter-wife, she's threatened that she may soon start creating tunes about *my* foibles."

Or, in a moment of 117 percent syrupiness, "My wife's so charming and persuasive she could make the Devil don a halo."

But then comes the moment I flaunt my ignorance: "I didn't even know vaulting existed as a sport until my seven-year-old granddaughter, who apparently can grow taller while I'm standing there talking to her, climbed onto a horse's back and blew me away by doing those gymnastic exercises."

After scrutinizing a gossip website a few weeks ago, I jotted down, "Just found tidbits about Mya, Ciara and Kesha, three one-name singers I've never heard — or, in fact, heard *of.*"

Some Post-its are whimsical:

- "How do you really feel about kohlrabi?"
- "My grandkid the other day stupefied her mother by saying, 'Mommy, I'm stupefied.'"

And some are wholly unencumbered phrases or words I might remember someday to use in a column: "A mental gulag." "Critter-sitter." "My inner cubmaster." "Puleeeze." "Donna Quixote."

And then there are scads of items I don't know quite know what to do with:

- "'I-spy' moment causes me to question what I saw — red-haired guy jogging barefoot, and bare everything else, on sidewalk."
- "Random notion: How'd I feel if I told an actor to 'break a leg' and he or she did?"
- "War — does it just have three letters or is it really a four-letter word?"
- "Kick-the-bucket-list: Things to postpone until *after* I'm dead."

But, if forced at gunpoint to choose my favorite, the note I relate to best is a summation: "I'm an addict. Dependencies, in order of import, include my wife and kids and grandkids, my iMac (incongruously combined with being a Luddite), Diet Pepsi Wild Cherry, High-Tech burritos, films, jazz, taking digital photos and inserting prints into old-fashioned albums, and binge-watching *Law & Order* re-reruns."

Oh, I forgot: And Post-its.

Post-its redux: fresh looks at joy, irritation, nonsense

This column is a sequel. Call it Post-its 2.0.

Because hordes of folks told me they enjoyed the first one quite a while back, I've decided to follow up. And I don't think it matters that the three or four readers who bent my ear the most happen to be immediate family members.

What does count is that I have decomposing piles of judiciously composed material from which to choose.

In case you missed my original, I reported that my iMac was ringed with "instant reminders, to-do lists, and quick- or slow-witted brainstorms," and that "the yellow stickies also sit on my desk in three piles (do-it-now, do-it-asap, and fergettaboudit!)."

Still true. And it's kosher to plagiarize myself like that if I admit that's what I'm doing, right?

All of what follows got scribbled (more and more illegibly) onto Post-its in my recent past (which might actually mean a couple of years):

- From time to time my home gets transformed into a zoo — a coyote in the front yard, a turkey vulture reposing in a patio chair. No elephants or crocodiles yet, but, what the heck, I'm patient.

- With deepest apologies to Will Rogers, I've never met a sacred cow I *did* like.
- Attitude is everything. A dying friend once said, "Why let myself become glum over my situation? If I get depressed, it could spoil a whole day, and I don't know how many days I have left."
- A guy 10 years my junior called me "kiddo" the other day in a nearby park and it made me feel boyish.
- As my wife supervised her in another local park, my nine-year-old granddaughter was "picked up" by a boy. At that age, I guess, the operative line becomes "my playground or yours?"
- On life's inequities: I intermittently have a platinum mind and a tin ear.
- A man on a street leading to the next community informed two sidekicks, "My pooch never gets used to time changes. She insists on pooping to her own drummer — on DST, Doggie Standard Time."
- Didja ever realize that — unlike a computer keyboard — there's no undo button in life?
- A bejeweled matron at an ATM was gossiping to a friend: "I ate out with Margaret yesterday. She's always depressed. I sometimes think of our meals together as 'mercy munches.'"
- I'd love to go back in time — to the days when customer service reps were live human beings, not recorded prompts.
- My spouse, who knows me best, claims I'm "a wind-up Woody, whirring and whirling all the time." Wonder if her alliteration means something.

- A recent report warns that statin drugs can cause memory loss, but the data are ambiguous. Is that because the researchers couldn't remember what they found?
- I'm unsure how I feel about what a woman whose face and arms have become a lovely living sculpture of wrinkles muttered outside a drug store, "I still find it amazing that every new pain makes me disregard my old ones."
- Ever since I served for a year on the Marin County Civil Grand Jury, my favorite bumper sticker has been: Grand Jurors do it in secret.
- When younger, I never dreamed I'd hang with a batch of 70-year-olds someday. Well, today's that someday.
- I have faith that the governments of San Anselmo, Marin County, Sacramento, and Washington — regardless how ineffectual they get — will never be subject to a military coup d'etat.
- SUVs continue to be the bullies of the roadways.
- Since I pay my taxes in full, and parking tickets as well, I despise amnesty programs that gave delinquents a big break.
- I take it for granted that as long as I'm breathing, I'll be able to put one word after another and that most of them will mostly make sense. Please tell me I'm right.
- My granddaughter doesn't mince words: "I want it," she says. "Wow, there are so many things in this world that I want." I not only understand, I second her notion.

Snippets of conversations beguile, titillate, and shock

Unlike countless other organizations, I do no surveillance — electronic or other. Unlike cable news networks and Wikipedia, I don't spread misinformation, gossip, or rumors.

But I do grab snippets of tête-à-têtes from restaurants, park benches, and street corners. And, because what I overhear might end up as fodder for a column, I typically jot down what I snatch. Perhaps these delicacies will beguile, titillate, or shock you — maybe even as much as they did me. Check them out:

Says a teen girl in the hospital lobby, "I'm done with him. He's now just a speck in my litter box of life."

Outside a supermarket, a sly old man declares — albeit a little too publicly — to his vastly younger female companion, "I have a feeling some prankster put crushed Viagra in my miso soup at lunch."

A long-haired, college-age guy philosophizes outside a bike shop: "We all know what to do about Killer Bees, but how can we handle Killer Sharks — you know, those anti-middle-class Wall Street venture-capitalist types, or the Killer Publicists, the marketers who clutter up popular films with irrelevant product placements, or Killer Second

Amendmenters, those pro-gun jerks who think every kid's room should be stocked with an Uzi?"

While querying the town's building inspector about a new neighbor's construction project, I overhear another municipal employee say, "I absolutely need to unwind, un-stress, and un-overload."

I definitely can share a titter with the gray-haired gent in pristine white shirt, power tie, filthy sneakers, and tattered jeans in a public library branch who proclaims, "I love it that I'm old enough to still appreciate — in the face of all this damned technology — paper clips, rubber bands, and a plunger."

Addressing a diner who'd obviously over-tipped, an elated server in an upscale eatery raves, "Grazie, merci, danke, arigatou, toda, and asante. Oh, I forgot — thanks a lot."

A dowager in deep blue dress, diamond necklace, and studs outside a local yogurt shop laps up some vanilla one sunny p.m. "I'm supporting [two candidates]," she says, "and have donated to both their campaigns. I'm also speaking for them locally, sort of reversing things by putting my mouth where my money is."

One mid-lifer in front of the local police station states to another, "Arguing with a spouse is like having a nuclear war — nobody wins."

I hear, in the Post Office, a sentence that could never apply to a compulsive-obsessive neatnik, maker of priority lists, and lint picker-upper like me: "He's having a real romance with disorder."

But I completely agree with the disheveled mother who chides her ear-budded son outside a music store, "Once there were songs; now there's only noise."

Decked-out matron watching road construction with a gal-pal: "These days, more than ever, perseverance trumps perspiration."

Cynical older adult in a natural foods store generalizes un-originally, "Those that can, do; those that can't become politicians."

A twenty-something father, near a stone dinosaur at a park, appears to be wasting some psychology on his unmoving toddler daughter, "Okay, don't have fun. Don't have *any* fun."

Matronly blonde outside a bank waves her arms in a friend's face: "Our government has definitely completed its wrong-headed transition from the Gold Standard to an Ink Standard. The only question remaining is: How much money can the Fed print?"

A young guy with an unusually high forehead collars a sidekick at the local high school, "There's only one word to describe her — feckless."

Loaded down with books on a community college campus, a student chats with his clingy girlfriend: "A few minutes ago, John was quoting *The Huffington Post*, then *Wikipedia*. That's cool. But I'm still hoping he'll really go retro and quote *Esquire* or *Elle*."

Finally, while munching on a delicacy in a burrito shop, a millennial says to a worker cleaning tables, "Would your family be the basis of a soap opera, sitcom, or reality show? Mine could be all three."

Phony-baloney items? Nope – funny, touching, odd eavesdroppings

I've been a professional journalist for six decades so my penchant for eavesdropping and snooping has probably become a permanent occupational hazard.

Even if you diss me for it, I'm apt to retain my proclivity for overhearing people's private utterances and repeating snatches. Whether they're funny, touching, or odd. I'm especially thankful for their giving me a chance to construct columns like this.

Here, then, are samples of what I've savored during the last year or so, with not a single smidgeon of a phony-baloney item in sight:

At a pooch park, a disheveled guy says to a buddy: "I get really upset when my dog keeps barking at the same time my wife is barking orders at me."

A teenaged girl chatting with another outside a high school: "Boy, am I exhausted. I really overachieved today."

Exceptionally wrinkled woman at an upscale supermarket comments to an exceptionally unwrinkled male, "She's mourning the loss of a tight body. She says her derriere used to be like a cupcake but now's like a pancake."

A girl outside a school: "I wasn't happy all those winter rains made a snail decide to share my bathtub with me."

Man leaning on a cane decorated with ivory at an arboretum laments to a woman using a similar walking stick, "The Golden Years tarnish easily."

Balding man in a parking lot growls to a female exiting his car, "She has a black hole in her personality."

In a checkout line at a Dollar Tree store, an elderly woman complains of her widowhood, then tells a friend, "I'd like a guy in my life, but I don't want to be a nurse or a purse."

Says one elegantly dressed matron to a second in the Post Office, "I don't mind dying poor, but I don't want to live poor."

A blue-haired woman to a downtown gal-pal, "He's dangerous, like a human pit bull."

Smiling Asian girl waiting to be picked up by her mom at an elementary school: "He's enormous yet graceful, sort of like a gazellephant."

Says a young lady shopper in Costco: "His verbal jabs hurt a little — like breaking in a new pair of shoes."

"I definitely suffer from FOMO, the fear of missing out," says a young boy to a non-talkative tree while lying on a patch of grass on a baseball field.

One macho-looking stud to another outside a fitness center: "He's become wussified."

A diner on her cell phone at a sidewalk table outside a restaurant: "Tell her I'll be there in three bites."

"Our relationship is great because we can laugh at our foibles, laugh at our failures, laugh period," says a midlife fellow with red hair entering a night club one evening.

A smart-alecky, college-age punster in the local library asks while taking out a book, "If your mother monitors your every activity, does that make her a momitor?"

Woman muttering to herself as she enters a municipal hall: "Even angels can have soiled wings."

Whispers an old-timer to his female companion outside a drug store: "I just filled out a Do Not Resuscitate form. I don't want to be a broccoli."

Finally, I catch one of my neighbors pleading with his dog (who was barking at deer in his front yard): "Hey, stop your yipping. They're allowed. We've agreed the bucks can stop here."

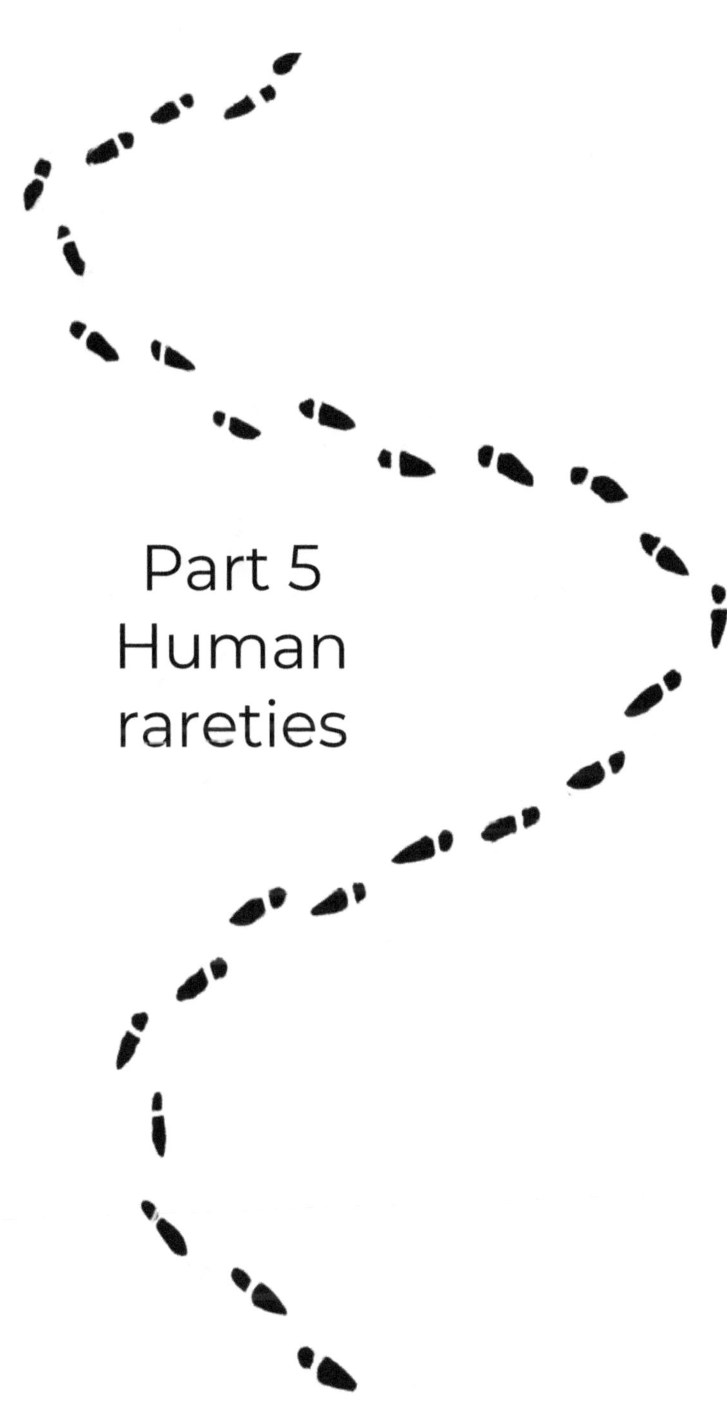

Part 5
Human rareties

Cambodian refugee works her dream after surviving slave-labor camp

Sophie Lim almost starved to death as a teenager in a slave-labor camp, every day for four years in the late 1970s.

She was fed only bits of watery rice under the yoke of the murderous Khmer Rouge in Cambodia. Her weight plunged to 70 pounds. "I was all bones and skin," she remembers.

After being hospitalized for four months, then forced to return to toiling 10 to 14 hours every day in mud-filled rice paddies, Sophie escaped "with a delivery guy who had two oxen pulling a wagon." Sighing, she tells me, "I'm lucky I survived. About 1.7 million died" — from starvation and the infamous genocidal killing fields.

We're sitting at a table in an upscale shopping center in San Anselmo, soaking up sun near Sophie's Nail Spa, a salon she owns. She also owns her home across the bridge in Richmond, another house in a city close to Sacramento, and two rental structures in nearby Oakland. Regardless, the 57-year-old immigrant whose ambition, energy, and hard work helped her achieve the American Dream feels compelled to work 10 to 12 hours a day.

But that's a long way from being awakened at 3 a.m. and being made "to walk a mile or two, sometimes more" to the work fields in a country where she'd been torn from her mother and sister (her father died when she was six). It's also a long way from being obliged to listen nightly at 7 "to a brainwashing meeting."

Her captors, she says, "were killing people, making them disappear, but they made it sound like they were doing good things. We knew better."

The Khmer Rouge, Communist offshoot of the Vietnam People's Army from North Vietnam, had galvanized a system of torture and executions that melded with widespread famine stemming from its failed attempts at agricultural reform.

The nightmare will always haunt her. "Hundreds slept together, with only room for you and your mosquito net. You made friends with people you worked with, but mostly you didn't trust anybody."

If you got sick, you first were sent to "a clinic where there was no doctor. They just gave you an IV, putting young coconut juice into your veins."

Nowadays Sophie tries not thinking about everyone stealing food to survive even though "if you stole and they found out, they killed you."

Nor does she often ponder doing without: "No shoes, no toothbrush, nothing."

But the memories spur her to give back by donating money to help Cambodia's poor. Often.

Sophie initially returned to Cambodia in 1999 and has visited half a dozen times since. "I helped build a Buddhist temple, after collecting money from the Cambodian community and adding some of my own," she reports. She also raised funds "to dig wells for two villages."

Not all memories of her native land are negative. One bright spot was meeting her husband "in the street" shortly after her escape. A year later, they wed. A year after that, they came to Oakland despite neither speaking a word of English. "We learned by watching a lot of *Sesame Street*."

In 1983, at age 24, she found an assembly line job she kept for a year (until the company went bankrupt). Three years later, she gave birth to her second son (she also has a daughter) and started cleaning houses. She did that for a decade.

Sophie and her husband had also adopted a Cambodian orphan, bringing him with them when they emigrated.

Eventually she bought what's now Sophie's Nail Spa — 19 years ago.

Her life wasn't trouble-free during the ensuing tenure, however. Her daughter, now living in housing under the auspices of a mental-health program, was "diagnosed at age 18 with schizophrenia" in 2002. Sophie's carpenter husband "quit his job to take care of her." But he died seven years later from liver cancer, after a $300,000 transplant. Sophie carried his ashes back to Cambodia, where she built a shrine.

Today she loves it here, living and working her dream. "I'm happy a lot, laughing all the time. I'm not a grumpy person no matter what happens."

When I ask about the government's current anti-refugee stance, she replies, "I don't like [it]. People should be able to come here and help people back home. There's no place like America."

She says it's crucial to give refugees hope, something she'd lost repeatedly in the slave-labor camp.

What's possible? Just ask the developmentally disabled dynamo

Kellie Greenwald stands less than five feet tall in her socks. But she's a human dynamo — witty, charming, artistic, a community college graduate, and an author.

Oh, yeah, I almost forgot: She has Down syndrome.

Kellie, writer and illustrator of *Kellie's Book: The Art of the Possible*, tends to grin a lot. I find it nearly impossible to talk with her and not do the same.

I attend an autographing session of hers at a nearby Borders bookstore. It takes her only seconds to demonstrate what someone who gets early treatment can accomplish with a strong will. Then, with warmth and glee, she injects, "I'm famous."

Her father tells me, "She tends to say that from time to time. She thrives on the attention, loves to speak in public, more than anyone in the family."

He should know, since he's not exactly a slouch with the public: He's former San Francisco Giants' broadcaster Hank Greenwald, who claims "some people can work a room, Kellie could work a ballpark."

Hank resides in San Francisco; his 30-year-old daughter lives in an apartment at the Cedars of Marin, which has 18 suites for developmentally disabled adults in Ross, north of the Golden Gate. She says she "liked it when I lived in a group home, but I *love* it now, independent and on my own."

She also thrives on becoming a role model, speaking before grammar school kids, taking part in a promotional TV shoot, being asked to do a workshop at a school for the deaf, and doing book-signings as far away as Florida.

Lisa Scandurra, arts program director at the Victory Center for Arts and Communications, where Kellie worked two years on her book, contends that "she's a wonderful spokesperson for people with Down syndrome."

Wikipedia explains that the chromosomal disorder, which occurs every 800 to 1,000 births, is frequently "associated with some impairment of cognitive ability and physical growth as well as facial appearance." A single glance reveals Kellie's condition. But when I chat with her, I immediately see she has realized the "possible" of her book's title.

Part of her abilities stem from her mother, Carla, having carried her less than three weeks after birth to an infant development program for physical and occupational therapy where they "believed in her potential, not her limitations." Kellie then learned sign language; reading and writing from a speech therapist; and was "mainstreamed" in elementary and high school, living at home until she was 18. She subsequently moved to Lifehouse, a group home.

She was employed for a while at a local drug store and then at a café. And she's been doing art for about eight years.

Along the way, she attended about 400 Giants games (and even traveled to spring training). Because she's such a fan, Kellie's thinking about doing a second book ("about baseball"). Whether she'll use the same format as her first — brightly colored drawings and hand-lettered text (plus four pages of personal photos) — remains to be seen.

No matter what, she says, she plans to continue "writing about my feelings."

Kellie's interests seem broader than those of many young people I've met who squander countless hours via iPod or texting. "I like playing guitar, singing, writing in my journal," she says. "I also like swimming, playing golf, gymnastics, exercising."

She's grateful for the help she seeks and gets ("therapy, classes in art and drama"), pleased by being able to meet friends at a farmer's market Thursday evenings.

Her voice conveys her exhilaration. Lisa shares that effervescence and elaborates: "Kellie writes great poetry and stories, has a great sense of humor and a huge heart, a huge amount of compassion, and zest for life. She conducts herself with grace and decorum and gives those around her a joyous feeling."

Barbara Ray, who with her husband, Norman, published the 52-page hardcover, observes that "Kellie isn't judgmental, isn't critical, is very positive."

Her days are hardly free of bumps, however — the book even includes a drawing of a girl crying. "Sometimes I feel sad because I am confused, frustrated, and overwhelmed," she admits. Mostly, though, she's upbeat, "happy because it's time for me to get on with my life."

My 11-year-old grandson, who's artistically inclined and enjoys word play, isn't developmentally disabled. But I plunked down the requisite $24.95 to send him *Kellie's Book*, which just might propel him by example to greater achievements.

Come to think of it, my older grandson's a bit of a slacker and could use some inspiration, too. I think I'll buy a second copy.

Nonagenarian spearheads tributes to Rosie the Riveter

It's been two years since Phyllis Gould collected her 15 minutes of fame.

She remembers it like it was yesterday. But it's today and she's absorbed with further pushing the Rosie the Riveter brand.

Phyllis details her exploits for me in her Fairfax apartment. A scrapbook with photos of her with national and state leaders lies nearby, as does the current *Time* magazine. She's open. Direct. Sharp. And at ease in green shirt and blue slacks.

Unlike four other Northern Californians who flew with her to D.C. to be honored by President Barack Obama and Vice President Joe Biden, Phyllis no longer volunteers regularly at the waterfront Rosie visitor center-museum across the bridge in Richmond. But she does swim twice weekly, help out at a food pantry, and drive her 1988 stick-shift pickup.

The epitome of spunky. Despite being 94.

She's now busy nudging Congress to okay March 21 — within Women's History Month — as Rosie the Riveter Day. "It's gonna happen," she says. "I won't give up until it does, even though it was stuck in committee for over a year. I say, 'You guys are taking longer to do this than it did for us to build ships and planes.'"

After that task, she wants to prod the feds into minting a coin marking Rosie significance.

Then? When I ask what one thing she'd tackle if handed a magic wand, she doesn't hesitate: "Gun control. Something has to be done to stop military weapons from being available to everyone."

Phyllis, as usual, is rich with patience. Which is how she got to meet Obama, Biden & Co. and, along with the other Rosies, be featured on *Good Morning America*. And be named grand marshal of a festival parade — as well as be cited by her local town council for being "an inspiration to women and girls today."

The nonagenarian's fame climaxed her tenacious 12-year letter-writing campaign. "All the military had monuments and recognition and we didn't get any," Phyllis had told reporters, "and we're not going to be around that much longer."

But the letter that drew attention was one telling Biden she wanted a hug. Which she got — although Kay Morrison, a Rosie who'd joined her on the complimentary Virgin flight to Washington, may have fleetingly overshadowed that by planting a lip-kiss on Obama.

A Norman Rockwell painting showing a woman on lunch break with a rivet gun in her lap had spawned the Rosie moniker. The real Rosies brought the resultant image of a muscle-bound wench in overalls to life, albeit unheralded.

Phyllis likes recalling how she became one of the first six women to shatter the 1942 union glass-ceiling, starting as a 90-cent-an-hour journeyman welder at Richmond's Kaiser shipyards. She also revels in the memory of driving through every mainland state and, in the '80s, spending seven summers as a cook for Denali National Park staff in Alaska.

Before chatting with her, I'd toured the free Rosie visitor center, part of the World War II Home Front National Historical Park. That Friday, four Rosies were present, all near or past the 90-year mark. All spunky.

One was Marian Sousa, Phyllis' sister. "In four years, we built more than 700 ships," boasts the 90-year-old who'd learned to draw blueprints at the University of California at Berkeley so she could work as a draftsman. Not all was ideal, though. Kay recollects a "huge sign in the hiring hall: 'No women or blacks wanted.'"

She returned when the sign came down, becoming a journeyman welder. That was "73 years ago," she notes, but "we had equal pay for equal work."

Phyllis may never get a second bite of the celebrity apple, but her first will always carry a sweet residue — like rose petals pressed into a memory book — for her. Meanwhile, she'll forever remain in *my* memory bank. So, indeed, will the visitor center-museum, despite being hidden in an industrial area that's difficult to find.

My top takeaway? Having heard that Biden called the Rosie feats "the real start of the women's liberation movement," I suggest to Phyllis that a Hillary Clinton presidency might be the logical next step. Without missing a proverbial beat, she agrees — 100 percent.

Two feed the hungry, differently, as their hearts ache

Andrea Carla Michaels and Marv Zauderer take different approaches to the hungry. Both succeed.

One-to-one, Andrea's been handing slices of pizza to the homeless on San Francisco streets and alleys almost daily since Christmas Eve 2015; Marv feeds hundreds in Marin County each day via ExtraFood.org, an organization he founded in 2013.

Neither's ever gone without food — except, Marv jokes, "on Yom Kippur," a Jewish fast day — yet both feel compelled to help the helpless.

Andrea, 57 and a longtime friend who averages "about 20 re-warmed slices a day, with the most being about 40," has been dubbed by her recipients as The Pizza Lady.

Her deliveries began after seeing two Algerian Muslim eatery owners "composting a large pizza with only two slices missing because they weren't allowed, by law, to sell them beyond four hours after they were made."

She told them, "I'd be happy to hand it out to the hungry have-nots — the 'NOTs' being 'Neighbors On The Streets.'"

Andrea, also a Jew, follows the "precept of *tikkun olam*, healing a broken world."

Marv, 53, who's in his third career, has watched his organization mushroom. So far, 200 volunteers have picked up 982,000 pounds of food and delivered it to 84 sites serving Marin's "most vulnerable." That translates to 50,000 people in food pantries, homeless shelters, senior centers, and after-school programs, folks "worried about where their next meal's coming from."

He tells me that "when I've seen a child come to school hungry, or I've looked in the eyes of a homeless person at a soup kitchen, or I've heard from seniors having to choose between food and medication, I've felt so sad. And then I've felt angry. Because I know there is enough food for all."

Andrea and Marv certainly aren't alone when it comes to feeding the hungry. The SF-Marin Food Bank, for instance, serves hundreds and hundreds of families each week through its pantry network.

According to Irene Garcia, 33, a pantry coordinator, Marin residents alone are "missing nine million meals a year." She points specifically to "the silver tsunami that's happening here," and says the food bank "is hoping to meet the demand of our seniors in need."

My personal interest in the hungry dates to an Alaskan cruise several decades ago when I witnessed tons of food being dumped because of liability issues. Andrea and Marv agree that Good Samaritan laws now protect businesses. But legal shields don't kill suspicion. I was in Moscow a while back when a rabbi couldn't give away leftover kosher food because the homeless wouldn't trust it. Or him.

Andrea's heart aches regularly for the one-third of her recipients who are regulars — as well as for "the rest who change from day to day."

She recalls one dude in particular: "He disappeared, and the others thought he'd died so they held a memorial service for him. It turns out he'd been in a hospital for two months, after literally dying — his heart stopped — and being revived. Now he's on the same corner with his friends, although none had known his last name."

Marv, who grew up in a Silicon Valley home "where food was central to connecting people," notes that despite Marin largely being an affluent county, "there is so much hunger here it breaks my heart."

What ExtraFood.org does is recovery. "Normally, we pick up excess food and immediately deliver it," he explains. "However, many restaurants don't have excess. So, restaurants like Taqueria Mi Pueblo, through our planned giving program, make us 10-20 servings to deliver."

Andrea's road-less-traveled has been zig-zaggy.

An attractive, blue-eyed, curly-haired blonde Harvard grad, she did standup comedy and wrote sitcoms in Los Angeles, taught foreign students English, then moved to San Francisco in 1993. A quintessential wordsmith, she's tutored folks in *Scrabble* and constructed crossword puzzles for *The New York Times.* Solving a mystery phrase won her a motor home on *Wheel of Fortune.* She now runs a firm she began, Acme Naming, which brands products and businesses.

In a sense, however, she's obsessed with her pizza journey — and recalls "a man who insisted I take a beautiful but not valuable ring. I wear it every day to remind me that I'm married to the work."

Life for good-looking, gray-haired, and balding Marv, meanwhile, has been vastly more linear. He spent 20 years in the technology world, then became a psychotherapist for 14.

But now his focus is on the fact that "40 percent of all food in this country is wasted."

Two women who resisted the Nazis will never forget

Some things we should never forget. That the Holocaust *wasn't* limited to Jews, for instance, and that Jews *did* fight back.

We certainly must remember the six million dead. But the Nazis also killed millions of non-Jews — Soviet prisoners of war, Polish citizens, Gypsies, the disabled, political and religious dissenters, gays.

Decades ago, my first day as Managing Editor of the Jewish Bulletin of Northern California, a man who'd survived Auschwitz-Birkenau and four other World War II camps pleaded, "No matter what else you do, don't let anybody forget the Holocaust."

I never forgot him, or the slogan "Never forget!" — the rallying cry for Jews the world over.

But it was quite a while before I'd encounter anyone who'd joined the resistance. They, too, bear scars: physical, emotional.

Consider octogenarian Sonia Orbuch. She fought Nazis as a teen, part of a partisan unit whose mission was resistance and sabotage, including the mining of train tracks. She mostly was an impromptu field nurse, helping doctors amputate limbs, treating the wounded with skimpy supplies and blood-soaked bandages, and cradling the dying.

The Marin County resident can't forget the nightmare, or a brutal winter hiding in a Ukrainian forest. She lived fearfully "all the time" then, and knows she'll never forgive. "Even when it's a happy moment or a holiday…the pain is tremendous," she tells me.

In a book aimed at teenagers, she'd asserted that every day she mourns "my mother and two brothers, dozens of other relatives, and nearly all of my childhood friends."

But she also knows it's crucial to dispel the myth that Jews didn't resist the Nazis.

Her son, Paul, had solidified his own legacy by co-founding the Jewish Partisan Educational Foundation. It, he notes, is "seeking 100,000 teachers, Jewish and non-Jewish," to inspire new generations by showing "the history and life lessons of the Jewish partisans."

What's it like being a survivor's child? "I always go back to what Sonia's said, 'You have to stand up early against tyranny, oppression, discrimination, anti-Semitism, whenever and wherever it occurs, and you have to teach the kids.'"

Yet, even as his messages spread hope, others dispense hatred: The Associated Press reports a 30 percent worldwide surge in anti-Semitic violence and vandalism last year, economic nosedives again making Jews scapegoats.

Paul once told a Jewish community center audience about hearing Sonia's friends reminisce "about the war, their losses, and their survival experiences. They did so with tears and sometimes with humor. And almost always there was anger and the refrain…of 'never again.'"

His daughter, Eva, has recalled that she'd once told her bat mitzvah tutor she "understood what my grandmother had gone through. My tutor challenged me...and I came to realize...I may never be able to truly understand or feel what my family and millions of others endured. I will only be able to ask questions and grapple with my past."

Another resister, Paula Ross, just moved into a veterans' home.

The Vienna-born, 92-year-old can't forget either — how she fought with the resistance to retaliate: "They killed my uncles, aunts, cousins, and friends."

She still doesn't "like to talk about it, because it was very traumatic," but, despite misgivings, she returned to Austria two years ago "and taught teenagers about the Holocaust, telling them exactly what the Nazis did."

Morgan Blum is director of education for the Holocaust Center, part of Jewish Family and Children's Services in San Francisco. She says a survivor once was defined as someone who'd been in a death camp but now signifies "anyone who was targeted for death and survived."

That means they "may have been in an extermination camp, may have been a hidden child, may have been a partisan, may have fled in 1936."

Morgan recently gathered "600 students and teachers from 101 private, public, and parochial schools to participate in our annual Day of Learning. About 95 percent were not Jewish. Over 70 percent had never heard a survivor before, but meeting one, they could make a connection."

One attendee, after hearing about Rwandan, Cambodian, Bosnian, and Darfur genocides, vowed "to prevent this from happening again, to not be a bystander."

Another told Morgan it's critical "to carry on this story because the next generation won't be able to hear from a living survivor."

Yes, I too believe it's categorically imperative that survivor's stories survive.

Un-ordinary Joe pushes poetry, combats bullying

I'm ignorant about oh, so many things. Poetry may top the list.

So, it amazed me that I wanted to interview Joseph Zaccardi, Fairfax resident and Marin County's poet laureate.

Joe's scarcely the only poet in his town. There's also Kay Ryan, Pulitzer Prize-winner and U.S. poet laureate whom Barack Obama just handed a major medal (along with filmmaker George Lucas, a resident of neighboring San Anselmo).

Can I deduce that poetry's as popular hereabouts as statues of Indiana Jones and Yoda that are standing tall — and short — in San Anselmo's Imagination Park, a rest-and-relax spot that Lucas donated? No way. But down-to-earth Joe Zaccardi conceivably could become the antidote for anti-poets.

His tips: "Don't be afraid of poetry. You have to cultivate a taste for it. Read widely. Try writing free verse — you'll surprise yourself. You'll find yourself writing about love, or the death of someone. You'll remember something someone said. Or you might ask yourself a question, really off the wall, like, 'I wonder if they ever fried insects.'"

Of his work, the 65-year-old notes, "Every once in a while, my sense of humor slips into my poetry, and I leave it there. But I'm usually serious."

He cites as a solemn for-instance "Arroyo's Soul," a poem that emphasizes subject matter "that's really quite deep, about our not believing in anything anymore."

Joe's background isn't riddled, however, with the snooty posturing sometimes attributed to writers. For much of his life, after apprenticing as a butcher, he functioned as "a barber, not a stylist, and I used to tell people I do one style — it'll be shorter." He hung up scissors and combs in 2003.

Retirement means he now can take whatever time is necessary, rather than jotting down a word or two between clients. First drafts average 30 to 40 minutes. "Of every 10 of those, I only continue one or two" — and then his editing process "can be another month."

He's published 240 poems so far but is "sure I've written 1,000." *Written* is precise. Although he utilizes a computer for other tasks, he creates poems in longhand, in a notebook, in ink.

Joe gets $5,000 for his two-year stint as poet laureate, scarcely enough to buy writing materials. But the meager honorarium isn't the point: The position enables him not only to promote poetry but use the bully pulpit to stage a panel discussion on "bullying and bystanders."

He remembers being 13: "A fat kid was picked on at lunch every day. One day six guys were doing it. I'm not brave, but I stepped in front of him and said, 'Hit me instead.' The leader said, 'Let's leave them alone.' And I realized one person *could* make a difference."

While being a teenager, Joe — who last month married his longtime partner, Dave Eng — also recognized he was gay.

A teacher concurrently spurred his interest in poetry through William Carlos Williams, a New Jersey native like Joe, and advised him not to worry about punctuation marks or rhymes. At 25, though, he started punctuating. "Now I love it," he says jocularly, "especially semi-colons."

Today he's drawn to Jane Hirshfield of nearby Mill Valley, Pablo Neruda, Gerald Stern, "and lots of Chinese poets." Earlier favorites? Shakespeare, Chaucer, and Allen Ginsberg.

Ginsberg, in fact, had hit on him. "I was in my 20s and I met him. He bought me a Heineken's beer, put his hand on my leg and said, 'You have very nice thighs,' and I said, 'The thigh's the limit.'"

Joe snickers at both pun and memory.

Actually, the skinny, six-foot poet is *totally* animated when speaking. His hands perpetually move, and he occasionally jabs a finger at something invisible. Off and on go his wire-rimmed eyeglasses.

His soulful eyes remind me of actor Steve Buscemi's. "They used to be brown but now they look gray, really strange," Joe comments, noting that as a schoolboy he asked a nun what color Jesus' eyes were. "The color of yours, I'm sure," she replied.

Since the early '80s, he's been hanging out at the Marin Poetry Center, which "puts on monthly sessions with visiting poets, an open mic once a month, and a wonderful thing called the Summer Traveling Show, which sponsors about 125 readings in various venues."

He likes reading aloud: "You can feel an audience when you read a poem."

When, at his request, I audibly read one — about his father, from his anthology, *Render* — I'm overwhelmed by its power. And I understand why he's a very special Joe, not an ordinary one.

Real men *do cry* – tears that might fend off violence

I'm an anomaly. Not only didn't I hear the stereotypical admonition "real men don't cry" as a boy, my father never tried to hide *his* tears.

Since Pop was my hero, I emulated him in many ways, sobbing included. "I'm such a softie," I've flippantly informed friends, "I cry at Road Runner cartoons." It's only a tiny exaggeration.

If I want an excuse to flood my tear ducts, I need only watch an old flick like *Field of Dreams* or *Marley & Me*.

I equate crying with vulnerability because my dad taught being open would make me healthier. Most dudes don't buy the concept.

I lead Marin Man to Man, a group for guys whose partners have had breast cancer and other life-threatening diseases. Although current attendees have no difficulty opening up about their shortcomings, new members are hard to attract. Despite their anguish, most guys outside the group are unwilling — or unable — to show feelings they perceive as weakness.

Lee Glickstein and Pete van Dyk believe men can overcome boyhood brainwashing. Together, they run Men of Tears, a workshop group featuring two-hour circles in which guys can seize their emotions and wash away chunks of anger, sadness, and fear that weighed them down for years.

When he realized he rarely cried, and hadn't wept at his mother and father's funerals, Lee, a communications coach/facilitator, started the group. "Crying can be eloquent," he tells me. "It may start as a rivulet, become a stream, then an ocean. We don't analyze it. We just want to experience and listen to the tears."

His best-case scenario? "Finding tears of self-compassion, giving permission to care for and be sweet to ourselves" — and maybe leading to what he calls "tears of humanity, tears of community, tears of possibility."

The tear-letting is no panacea, though: "I still don't have a full range of emotions," admits Lee, who lives in an unincorporated community near mine.

So far, Men of Tears has drawn Caucasian, African American, Hispanic, and Asian participants aged 19 to 69.

Most men, Pete assures me, rarely cry beyond age 10. He quit at 8. He'd seen *Old Yeller*, a film about a boy having to kill his dog. As he sobbed, his siblings insisted he "stop being a crybaby." That moment, he notes, "is pretty classic. Boys are often told, 'Be a man — don't cry," or threatened with, 'I'll give you something to cry about."

Society apparently hasn't changed: It has mockingly tagged John Boehner as "Weeper of the House."

But Pete, who for 17 years counseled and coached prisoners at San Quentin to face their feelings and be accountable for their actions, is hopeful. Working as violence-prevention manager with the Insight Prison Project, he endorses its motto: "Leaving prison *before* you get out" — a reference to constraints of both mind and emotions.

Impulses for violence, he explains, are outgrowths of emotional blockages stemming from societal pigeonholing. "Go into a toy store and the boys' section is filled with guns and GI Joe figures."

Pete, who now tracks his own tears on a daily basis, elaborates: "Not being in touch with emotions means we can't sit down and talk with each other, and that can set us up to be violent. Gang violence, religious violence, domestic violence, national violence such as war — it's all the same."

Kevin Penn, who became a counselor during his 24-year imprisonment, is one of Pete's success stories. "From the age of 11, maybe to 38, I had cried maybe 10 tears," Kevin reports, "and then my life started to change."

Bottled-up feelings consistently are to blame. According to Pete, they may lead to non-communication, which may lead to violence, the epitome of which is war.

One of his "best moments" in Men of Tears was when "a 19-year-old going into the military and an older man who'd gone to the Air Force Academy talked about getting in touch with their emotions as a way to avoid the Post-Traumatic Stress Syndrome that's so prevalent."

But "how can we have spent three trillion dollars for wars in Iraq and Afghanistan," he asks me rhetorically, "and not have enough to pay for social programs?"

And yet, I suppose if we follow the "real men *do* cry" tenet to its logical conclusion, we could also project an *end* to war.

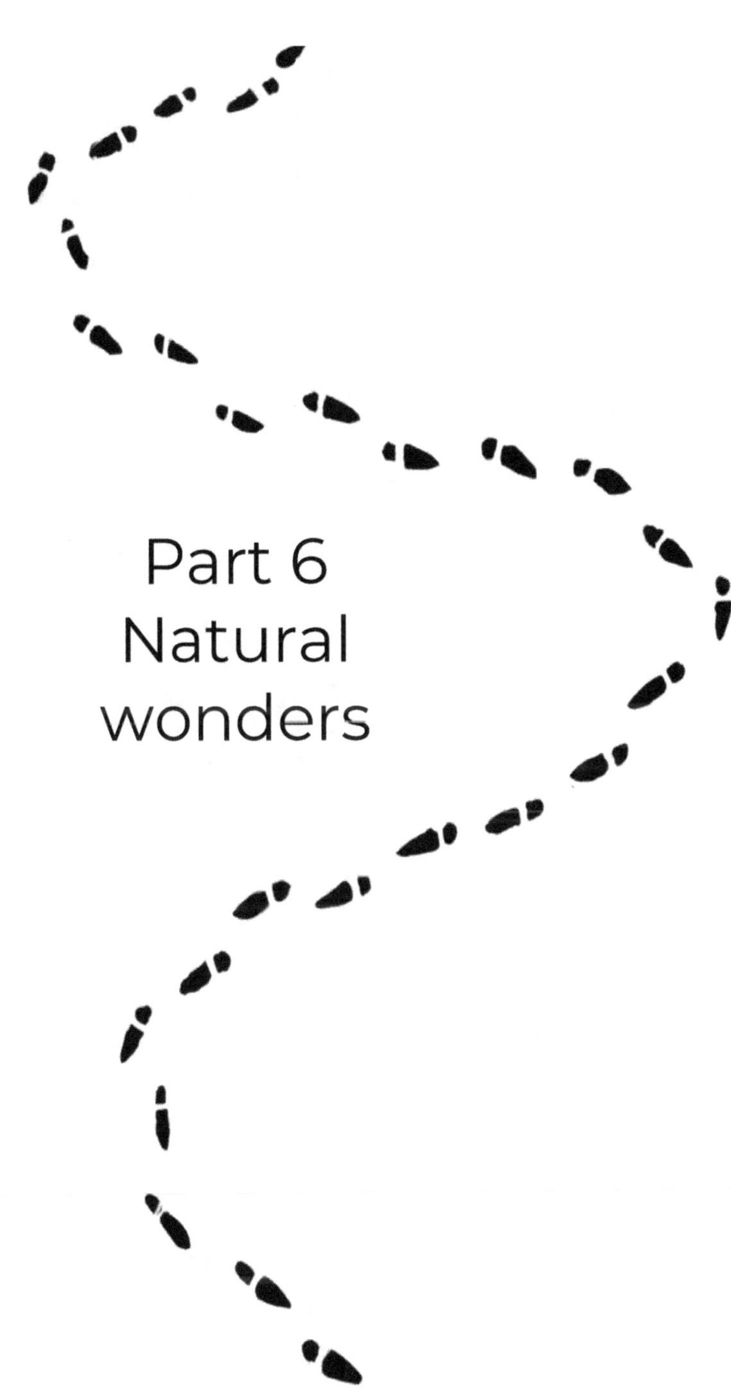

Part 6 Natural wonders

Writer witnesses woodsy, weird, whimsical wildlife

My wife and I live on the edge of the woods, atop a steep hill. It's frequently like being part of a Discovery Channel program.

When we first moved in 22 years ago, we planted about $1,800 worth of foliage. A latter-day Bambi and her extended family didn't know the nursery salesman had sworn the greenery would be deer-resistant, so they devoured every last "hors d'oeuvre" within a week.

We decided to leave the place rustic.

It took less than another week for us to be awakened, in the ebony of a starless night, by the unnerving screeches of a food-chain episode featuring unidentified critters just outside the French doors of our bedroom. Not many days later we saw a hawk swoop into our back yard to clutch a snake in its mouth and fly off toward the nearby seminary.

As I look back at those events from the vantage point of a presidential year, I recognize there's nothing out of the ordinary about one animal wanting to obliterate another (even bipeds of either gender).

And in the spirit of full disclosure, my wife and I — despite having long been staunch environmentalists — have had few qualms about hiring a pest control guy to ambush a legion of carpenter ants or an invading rat or three (despite their subsequent stink and despite our having totally enjoyed *Ratatouille*, the animated Pixar film).

But we'd rather remember repeatedly finding ourselves spellbound watching a cornucopia of wildlife in our unplanned sanctuary. Highlights include:

- A skinny green reptile — whom we dubbed Eddie Lizard after the English actor-comedian — crawled out of its skin right before our eyes.
- A bobcat crouched in the bushes an excruciatingly long time after it jumped from a tree in our driveway next to the car my wife and dog were riding in. The windows stayed up a long time.
- Two swallows built a nest in our eaves but argued about where it should be situated, the male obviously wanting a room with a view, the female so insistent on a protected space in a corner that she tossed away the twigs he'd collected until he conceded.

That, however, is only scratching the naturalist surface in our environment.

- Three different skunks (from a suburban family that thrives in a drainage ditch down the road) "anointed" our pooch on three separate occasions because she got too nosy about their sightseeing outings.
- A pair of athletic gray foxes disrupted our dreams by noisily playing tag on the main deck outside our living room one moonlit midnight. We couldn't tell which one was "it."
- A slew of wild turkeys (including an astoundingly wrinkled fellow we nicknamed The Big Pecker because he clearly led the pecking order) painted almost all of that deck with bird droppings.

- A squirrel auditioned a shaky high-wire act, its tiny right feet clinging to one electric company line on the side of our house, its left ones grabbing another a few inches away.

Over the years as the sun warmed our cul de sac, a multitude of scorpions crept out of our woodpile (one at a time, thankfully, precluding serial nightmares), a gang of slugs decided our walkway was the ideal vacation spot (they, too, joyously marched single file), and countless spiders sought refuge from storms in our shower (and were gently evacuated in a cup by my compassionate spouse).

In addition:

- Hundreds of cawing crows simultaneously discovered during their migration a big oak that hovers over our roof and blocks the distant lights of a shopping center. To us, they seemed to be improvising a remake of Alfred Hitchcock's *The Birds*.
- Once, voyeurism became our activity du jour as we spied two rabbits through our kitchen window living a cliché as they engaged in quickie matinee sex.
- A couple of quail awkwardly chased each other's tailfeathers on what would be our lawn were it not so weedy.
- A pair of young bucks crash-tested their emerging antlers on each other while a newborn fawn tried to stand for the first time on our hillside and tipped over because of the sharp angle. Tilt!
- While we luxuriated in our healing hot tub, we were also bathed by the harmonies of chirping birds in surround-sound — with two staccato woodpeckers acting as a rhythm section.

Myriad moons rose and faded, and all the while small armies of raccoons and possums and gophers, owls and doves and hummingbirds, butterflies and yellowjackets and assorted bugs couldn't care less that we might have craved a little bit of privacy on *their* home turf.

Our mini-wilderness varies just a tad from the nearby environs of my wife's daughter. She lives with a *domestic* menagerie — a dog, three goats, three barn cats, five horses, one guy and three kids.

But that's another story for another day.

To bee or not to bee, I learned to mingle with 5,000 of them

Ever since I was a toddler, bees have scared the bejeebers out of me.

So, I shocked myself when a friend and neighbor invited me to nose around in his hive. "Sure," I replied, thinking my report of it might make good reading.

Brian B. Beard — an outdoorsman with flaming red hair, mustache, and hazel eyes — became my mentor. And protector.

The backyard beekeeper duct-taped my trouser cuffs to my black sneakers. "Bees don't like dark shoes," he noted. "They'll think you're a bear."

He stuffed cloth beneath my chin where zippers met, to plug an unwanted hole. He safety-checked my white cotton bee-suit, netted face mask, and long rubber gloves. And he scrutinized honeybees flitting in and out of the 5,000-population hive so I could sidestep their flight path.

"There's practically no risk of your being stung," he said. "Bees aren't interested in you — unless you agitate them." Although my ears absorbed his words, my brain wasn't convinced. Ditto my fluttering heart and kneecaps.

Brian, who donned a bee-veiled hat to safeguard *his* face and neck, and gloves to shield *his* fingers and arms, remained fearless even when he dropped something and riled the flying insects.

I surprised myself by not freaking out as they zoomed all over me. Brian's words had been tranquilizers. It also didn't hurt that he'd engulfed me with bee-calming smoke.

I found myself fascinated watching bees enter the hive with pollen on their hind legs, seeing various stages of development (cells with eggs, larva, and pupae), tracing patterns of beeswax and honey. But disappointment surfaced when we couldn't locate the lone queen — or the drones, which Brian speculated had "already been pushed out of the hive because their only function is to mate."

I'd wanted my wife to document us photographically, but she flapped her hands as if warding off a swarm and said, "Are you out of your mind? I'm afraid." Instead, I recruited Brian's spouse, Kristen Gregoriev, who shot from a distance. She's allergic.

Not allergic to bees, or adventure, were three neighbor kids and their mom. The intrepid oldest offspring, a preteen, came within inches of the hive to snap a smartphone picture.

We all enjoyed identifying honey arcs. But I hadn't expected hearing wings of the virgin female worker bees, like Disney's seven dwarfs, whistling while they worked.

According to a supply catalogue, "If honeybees ceased to exist today, about one-third of all foods we eat would disappear…[Pollination allows] all flowering crops to reproduce. The outcome is fruit, vegetables, nuts and a wide variety of seeds…used for human and animal foods."

Brian, who's "been involved in nature since age one," touted Marin County Beekeepers for "information and camaraderie." That group's monthly meetings, said the 55-

year-old who does 100 push-ups each time he hikes up a nearby hill, draw more than 100 participants. Their website indicates how to become a beekeeper, and lists a queen-rearing project, meetings, classes, and speakers. The organization also helps when a swarm is discovered. "People call a fire department, and, usually within an hour, someone from the group will pick it up and re-hive the bees," Brian reported.

Why'd he begin beekeeping 14 years ago? "When I didn't have any in my garden," he said, "it seemed empty. To have a complete garden, you need bees. Besides, it's really fun to give someone a jar of super-fresh honey."

Another local resident, Mia Draper, wears an accolade tendered by others: "Queen Bee." Bees are definitely "wild creatures," she reported. "You have a better chance of herding cats. So, you must learn to work with them. To do right by them, we must attune ourselves to the cycle of nature. But when you find a new bee-plant, it can be as exciting as finding money in the street."

That certainly differs from alarmist views about Africanized bees. "Don't use the phrase killer-bees," Brian suggested, "because it's inaccurate and an exaggeration."

Not exaggerated are reports of bees dying. Scientists first noticed the mysterious disappearance of U.S. bee colonies in 2006. Two years later an annual count was launched to study declining pollinator populations and ecosystems that rely on them.

The jury's still out.

But honeybee hives are proliferating, even in the posh Waldorf-Astoria in New York City. Hoteliers hope to harvest their own honey and help pollinate plants. Guests can sign up for tours.

Maybe visitors there can have as much fun there as I did here. That, at least, is the buzz I'm peddling these days.

I find beauty in what surrounds me – instead of disasters

A nameless Greek dude observed, back in the third century BC, that beauty's in the eye of the beholder.

Plato paraphrased the fellah's words much later. And a slew of literary folks has repeated the notion ever since.

Well, for some unknown reason, my eye's been beholding one heck of a lot of natural beauty lately. Just the other a.m., for instance, I stepped onto my back deck and a post-sunrise sky-glow filled both eyes. I stared at the delicate oranges and pastel pinks and roses that oozed from unblemished ivory clouds, then gazed at the sliver of a moon still pasted on my right.

A celestial one-two punch. Hoo-hah!

Next, I gawked at my yard's lush green foliage — accented by patches of vibrant yellow daffodils and purple buds that punctuated our Vinca ground cover. I smiled, too, at the clusters of slinky white-trunked birches and 15-foot cacti that greet our visitors.

"Mega-beautiful," I mused aloud but to myself.

In back of our home, a century-old former hunting lodge, sat a bunch of violet flowers of undetermined origin, acting as a backdrop to the emerald moss that had materialized on a fallen tree. Yellow daisies poked their heads, meanwhile, from greenish beds in front of our dwelling, aka “The Shack.”

The mental picture-postcards were so beguiling they disabled my power of speech — an achievement my wife would claim is no mean feat.

Those 360-degree visuals also made me daydream about other beauty within sight, loveliness I could visit without difficulty.

I began with a nearby hill and the lone visible mountain, a striking contrast — the first one ravishing in its semi-nakedness, the near-distant peak divine in its mantle of foliage. The San Francisco Theological Seminary’s campus soon beckoned, with chapel towers nestled in trees that formed an earthbound yet heavenly choir when winds whistled between them. Then, ornamental pear and plum trees lining the main downtown avenue blew my polychromatic mind, their white blossoms as pure as the driven snows we never get here.

Miss Piggy, I decided, was wrong. Totally, even if her squeal was tongue-in-jowl: “Beauty is in the eye of the beholder, and it may be necessary from time to time to give a stupid or misinformed beholder a black eye.”

While pondering the serenely reflective waters of the creek that runs through our town, I recalled when they’d more than once risen so high that they overflowed and devastated businesses. Natural image? Yes. Beautiful? Not so much.

A friend dragged me out of a momentary mind-funk by citing nearby treasures — a local lake, the glorious open space of a welcoming rustic park. “And the higher you get, the more spectacular the view,” he maintained.

Extending my beauty-hunt to a neighboring community, I walk-wandered along a narrow street with resplendent greenery, ending up inspecting picturesque waterfalls and rolling hills from a municipal water district watershed. I heard a string of oohs and aahs. OMG, they were coming from me!

I've spent my adult life as a working journalist spotlighting society's underbelly: Natural disasters; man-made catastrophes, wars, and assorted mayhem; crimes and suffering; disease and pain; every imaginable evil. This was far better.

But it'd be impossible for me to scribble this column and exclude the most beauteous element of my life: Nancy Fox, a wife/soulmate/companion whose high cheekbones and fetching face attracted me more than 56 years ago — and still do. It's blissful that I can yet look past her wrinkles to the bewitching teenager I first met back east.

And that truth lets me forgive this ordinarily charismatic woman who in our winter bed transmutes into an ice cube and a heat-seeking missile that steals my body's warmth.

I guess that beauty, in the end, conjures up that old chestnut about art: I know what I like. But maybe I'm conning myself. Perhaps it's only what Kinky Friedman once roared, "Beauty is in the eye of the beer holder."

Ready to trade in my gas-guzzler to save the planet? Not yet

I try hard to be a good environmentalist. Really. And I often proselytize sustainability. To anyone in earshot.

If it appears that I'm apt to get a headache from wearing my halo too tight, or to sprain my arm patting myself on the back, you should know that according to more than a few of my fellow greenies, I fall way short.

When shopping, I do schlep assorted cloth bags into stores. But my brain aches trying to remember in which container to stash the plastic and tin and paper and batteries for recycling.

I buy my share of organics and support farmer's markets and local growing. And I do compost, though that needs a giant sanitary-service assist.

Sure, I seek out green businesses to support, and unplug or shut off electronic devices when they're not in use. While I yank out non-native species by the roots, however, I must be doing something wrong because the Scotch broom must be pulled again and again.

Environmental-me still uses water-saving techniques learned during Northern California's long-forgotten drought, sneers at Styrofoam carryout containers, and buys as little plastic as possible. I've also replaced incandescent bulbs with the squiggly ones that save energy, yet I gripe whenever they make me squint.

I pick up my dog's poop, even under thorny bushes, and now and then even scoop up other canines' "business." I shun single-use water bottles and other disposables yet strain to use reusable everything.

Yes, I've donated-recycled about a zillion items to Goodwill and humane society thrift shops and to homeless facilities. And some of the clothing I wear, even in public, is 40 years old.

Some environmentally conscious friends insist all that's not enough.

My ride, you see, is only half a dozen years old and it's a non-fuel-efficient, non-low-emission Camry, not an all-electric or hybrid car, not a bicycle. And certainly not roller skates.

Skaters Chantal Maher, Yvonne Roberts and Randy Hibbitts obviously do me one better.

Chantal, a tall woman who often uses her highly visible skating to promote environmental concepts, can be seen scurrying five days a week from home to a local cooperative nursery school where she's taught for 19 years. "The kids love to see me roll up," she tells me, "even though they're used to it. They especially enjoy seeing me twirl when I stop."

My colleague on the local Quality of Life Commission says she'll skate "to anywhere that's accessible unless it's pouring rain or if I have to carry too much. Not only has skating lowered my carbon footprint quite a bit, it takes less time — because of traffic."

Chantal, who's been skating since she was five, some 40 years ago, is loyal to "the old-fashioned kind, with four wheels, not roller blades." That's because they've become as comfortable as, well, an old shoe.

Yvonne, development and marketing director for a nearby "hub for healthy aging," has also been donning skates for four decades, though more for recreation. She heads an inline skaters' group of 40 roller-blading enthusiasts. "I'd love to get out of my car more often for environmental purposes," she asserts, "but it's challenging because of rough pavements."

Hills can be a problem, too.

Randy lives on one "that's fairly steep, making it a little hard to skate there." But he still believes it can be "a fun, efficient way to get from place to place without using any fuel except what we put into our bodies." Before moving into our small town a few miles north of the Golden Gate Bridge, he lived in San Francisco and commuted south to work via train. He roller-bladed from the station to his job, however, "an environmental approach." He's skated in local parades with his daughter and tells me his son stays mindful of the environment by bicycling to school.

All three are years younger than I and, to be honest, the notion of nose-diving off skates scares me a lot, even if I wore a helmet. So, I guess I'll just keep on doing the best I can environmentally and not try to save the planet by trading in my Toyota — a gas-guzzler, comparatively speaking — for at least another half dozen years.

Finding visible beauty instead of invisible men

It's 6:30 on a Tuesday morning that's as black as an oil spill off the Golden Gate. I'm driving from my home in search of a few guys who, it's rumored, watch the sun come up each day in Fairfax, a neighboring town just west of me.

When I get to the Little League field where they're supposed to be, not far from a park, nothing's stirring except a dozen crows strutting leisurely across the outfield.

The ballfield has been neatly trimmed, the base paths carefully rolled. Comprising a nearby still life are two weather-beaten benches, a shiny white plastic chair, a metallic water fountain, and a dispenser for degradable plastic bags for dog doo-doo.

Overall, it's a portrait in serenity.

Within minutes, however, countless birds chirp and warble, almost drowning out the sounds of early traffic on the main street.

A middle-aged, brown-skinned man in sweats and a blue and yellow windbreaker with a Michigan logo on the back starts his stretching. I ask if he knows about the sunrise group. "No," he says. "I exercise here every day and I've never seen then."

I wait. Nobody else materializes.

The first hint of a sunrise appears, replete with streaky palette of reds and pinks and yellows. In the background sits a pastel blue sky. A handful of delicate clouds floats by.

My mind wanders back to childhood, when I lay many afternoons on a hill near my suburban New York home and turned puffy white clouds into a vast menagerie; to young adulthood, when I watched majestic sunsets from cliffs overlooking Acapulco waters; to midlife, when I soaked up the pristine beauty of the Alaskan landscape; to recently, when I reveled in the rain forests of the Amazon and saw hundreds of varieties of exotic orchids in Peruvian gardens.

Splendor. Nature at its finest.

Here, though, my reverie is disrupted by a fellow with a Marines buzz-cut clunking a duffel bag onto the street while waiting to get picked up. I walk over and ask, "Have you heard of some guys, maybe old hippies, who watch sunrises from the ballpark?" "Nope," he replies. "Never heard of 'em."'

I return to the benches and watch the sun's rays spread, the hues brightening with each passing second. It's not the most spectacular sunrise I've ever seen, but it's excellent. Lovely.

The memories flash back — to the first times I'd glimpsed some of the nearby wonderment. A small, trickling waterfall hidden by the back roads. Rolling hills. San Francisco Bay, lit up by Fourth of July fireworks as seen from my adopted county. Whales swimming off the Pacific. The sole viewable mountain. And, of course, the majestic redwoods of Muir Woods.

The sunrise is fading, but my inner warmth isn't going to disappear quickly.

An androgynous guy with long dirty blond hair tucked into a cowboy hat strolls by, hot coffee in hand, dog trotting alongside. "Do you know if there are some fellows who watch the sun come up around here?" "Why do you want to know?" he snarls. "Because I think it would be an interesting pastime and I'd like to write a column about it," I answer. "I have no idea," he says, and moves off.

His dog doesn't indicate he knows anything about any gang of sunrisers either.

Minutes later, at 7:30, a couple with matching hounds come by. My question is automatic: "Have you ever seen some guys who watch the sunrise?" "That's way before we get up," says the male, a lot more cheerfully than the last interviewee.

I decide to return home, to decide whether to try to find the invisible guys again, and to walk my own dog in what appears to be developing into a remarkably balmy day.

Miniature signs naming the flowers planted in rows along the fence to the field that's been there since 1957 catch my attention. Some are blooming; some, like the guys I've been searching for, are nowhere to be seen. California lilacs. Coffee berry. Hummingbird sage. Western red bud. Oregon grape. Manzanitas.

I climb down the few stone steps from the field to the adjacent lot where I'd left my car. Having been sensitized to the total environment, I notice bumper stickers on the 16 vehicles now parked there. One on an old convertible with a heavily patched top and rusting body grabs my attention: "Save Fairfax." So does the skinny one on a red hatchback that proclaims, "May Peace Prevail on Earth."

Driving out, I pause at the lengthy, curved wall with colorful murals that encompasses the front of the ballfield, and am taken in particular with one titled, in part, "Tribute to Life."

Naturally.

Part 7 Amazing wife

White keys, black keys, nostalgia, and magic

Literary showoff Norman Mailer had the chutzpah to write a book titled *Advertisements for Myself.*

I'd never have the temerity to try anything like that. But I do have the courage to offer a paean for my wife. She's earned it, and not only for putting up with my husbandly idiosyncrasies for three decades.

Nancy Fox has cascading red locks, freckles, a slightly crooked smile, and a perma-twinkle in her hazel eyes.

I first fell for her when she was 16 and visiting New York state, then again 28 years later in California after both our marriages had dissipated. This year she'll turn 70, having long ago found the key to making my love grow daily.

But I'm hardly alone: Tons of Marin County gray-hairs adore her. Because she interacts with imps and grouches alike. Because she constantly reinvents tunes playing by ear, a talent since age 3. Because she has a sense of humor twice the size of Detroit, from which she insists she "escaped early."

My friend/partner/spouse regularly offers "piano and patter" at dozens of senior facilities. Venues range from locales where those with dementia sadly can't remember their children's faces to carefree spots in which residents prance daily in Sunday finery.

She radiates when listeners tell her she "makes us smile and gets our toes tapping." But it's the awakenings that really electrify.

During one program, a 92-year-old started singing "O Sole Mio," the first sounds she'd uttered in months. In another place, a man with Alzheimer's whistled as Nancy performed. "He hadn't done it for years," she says, "but something I did got to him and stimulated his whistling gland."

At a small group home close to where we live, she recalls, "I got requests for songs I hadn't played in decades, but my fingers hadn't forgotten. It's wonderful to watch faces light up with recognition. Some even get up and start dancing."

Many such instances have occurred over the years. "I've seen residents get so excited they dance with their walkers or move any part of their bodies they can in their wheelchairs," says Nancy.

But gigs like that fill only part of my wife's musical time. She recently played sedately for a convention of female venture capitalists. In contrast, she bubbles when backing a jazz singer, Joan Getz, for pro-bono recitals sponsored by Bread & Roses, a local charity founded by singer Joan Baez's sister, Mimi Fariña.

She also devotes one day a week to our two-year-old granddaughter, who lives half an hour away and who just learned the potty isn't a dollhouse.

No longer does Nancy do puppetry or teach kids. And rarely can she find the hours needed to compose with me (though we did finish a musical-comedy revue about aging).

Meanwhile, at the senior facilities, Nancy cloaks herself in nostalgia.

Her specialty is tunes from the '20s, '30s and '40s, melodies learned playing with her dad, Joe Falk, a big-band musician who played 21 instruments and sat in with the Dorsey Brothers, Paul Whiteman, and Peter Duchin. "I look at my hands," she notes, "and they look just like my father's. I appreciate the gift he gave to me, so I make it a point at every gig to play one of the songs he taught me."

Her repertoire — thousands of tunes, none played the same way twice — inspires reminiscences galore. At one spot, for instance, "a guy always asks for 'Sentimental Journey' because it was the song of hope for soldiers in World War II and takes him back to a time when he came home from the fighting."

Nancy plays on concert-size Steinway baby grands as well as "some of the funkiest keyboards on the planet, with keys that are broken or missing or sticky from mysterious gelatinous foods." She sits on stools ranging from those padded with leather to collapsible beach chairs fattened with several pillows.

A favorite anecdote depicts an instrument whose loose legs fell off, one at a time, over several months. "The keyboard finally was put on a moveable dolly, but the brake didn't hold, and I found myself playing a rolling piano headed for a wall."

She also good-naturedly flashes back to the woman on a stretcher who started shouting, "This is it — this is the kind of music I hate."

Nancy recollects, too, when a program "was interrupted by a fire alarm and the residents were scooted into another room. I started an impromptu sing-along."

Sentimentality is never far removed. In one place, a man asked for "Always," which he'd sung to his wife when they'd wed 50 years before. "What I didn't realize was that she was sitting in a wheelchair next to him, beaming."

Not everyone sits. Residents often join her after explaining they've been Broadway stars or professional opera singers or Rockettes.

In the final analysis, though, my wife particularly loves playing for those "whose memories are mostly erased but whose musical memories are somehow magically intact and can be reignited."

And in the process, she's creating new memories of her own.

Overcoming both hearing loss and bullying

"What?" "Would you repeat that; I didn't hear you." "Spell it, please."

I've heard those phrases again and again from my wife.

Seven or eight years ago, quite some time after she'd begun dying the gray out of her red locks, Nancy realized she was missing about every fourth word — even in the relative quiet of our home. So, she bought hearing aids.

I bristled at the cost, despite their being only mid-level pricey, and was acutely ticked off at the insurance industry for failing to cover even a penny. But the devices helped tremendously, except in trendy restaurants where decibel counts can approach that of a sonic boom.

Recently, though, Nancy's hearing ability shriveled some more. It was time to upgrade.

After road-testing several thingamabobs, she settled on what we wincingly called "the Rolls Royce of hearing aids." The tiny inserts actually cost way more than my first car, about a third of what I shelled out for my first house. The major upside, however, is that they work.

Hearing loss typically is linked with the elderly — and my wife snugly fits into that pigeonhole. The disability, though, is hardly limited to geezers. It can strike at birth.

Patricia Sirianni is certainly the proof in that particular pudding. She not only had to overcome being hard of hearing but childhood bullying as well — predictable slings and arrows that came with the condition. By age six on the East Coast, she'd learned to sign.

Now she can boast about having taught classes in American Sign Language at a community college for more than two decades. ASL, she explains to me through her amplified home phone, "is a visual, picture-form of communication" that merges facial expression, body language, and hand movements.

"Being a hard-of-hearing person myself," she says, she feels particularly qualified to use signing to show "how to convey emotional feelings, actions, ideas, the whole range of human communication." She invites students "into a world where you 'hear' with your eyes."

Each summer, Pat puts her theory into practice — on Mount Tamalpais, for Mill Valley's musical Mountain Play. This season, the theater's centennial, will be her 33rd there, signing the first three of six performances. "To prepare, I try to go to all the dialogue rehearsals," she says. There she learns to fit "the grass and trees and story" into an ASL format so she can project them.

"It's not English. I don't translate prepositions. But my hands do the words, my facial expressions show the actions and emotions — happy, sad — and my body moves to the beat of the music and shows it to the audience."

She's not sure how many deaf or hard-of-hearing folks watch her, but she's certain they enjoy the shows. "They sway back and forth, both to the vibrations and to my signing."

Pat's also interpreted for Youth in Arts, AA meetings, the St. Benedict Parish for the Deaf in San Francisco, and boys' and girls' high schools in that city. Mountain Plays differ from those classes and one-on-one sessions because she wears headphones that allow her to hear performers and musicians.

My wife, a professional musician herself, was terrified to admit her terror of what might follow hearing loss — an inability to play piano. She categorically had no desire to simulate a deaf Ludwig van Beethoven by picking up vibrations from a legless instrument placed flat on the floor.

The new aids, therefore, make her happy. Now she can even hear people coming up behind her — a good defense against purse-snatchers, I guess. Most importantly, she hears every note. She proves it by repeatedly playing my favorite tunes. And when she performs "My Funny Valentine" — "our song" — it's pure ear candy.

Although Pat can't forget her difficult childhood — when "the kids made fun of me" — she, like Nancy, is upbeat these days, and philosophical. She drills students who are struggling that they "can do it, even if it takes a lot more work."

It doesn't matter "what disability you have," she tells me, "you can always find a way to be successful, to reach the moon and stars."

My wife and I prefer not to think about everything we've lost

My wife keeps me busy by endlessly assigning me unwanted tasks.

Like finding her lost cell phone. And umbrellas. My search parties are mobilized weekly.

Not long ago, she phoned from downtown while walking our little white mutt. No, she hadn't misplaced our biodegradable poop bags. "Please come and rescue me," she wailed. "I've lost my keys again."

I scoured virtually every inch of her trail — two parks, block after block of the main avenue. I pushed aside foliage where Kismet had deposited some stinky stuff and Nancy had bent over to collect it. I checked each early-blooming flower, each parked vehicle. I kicked aside fallen leaves that had accumulated at curbside. I stopped counting at 1,439,574.

Diddly squat.

Happily, a young lad found the keys soon after we'd retreated to our home. He turned them into the police, whom we'd been smart enough to notify.

Losing this 'n' that has for sure become too habitual for both of us. As well as for a multiplicity of our aging friends. On a whim, Nancy and I crafted a list — and noticed that losing something isn't necessarily bad. When she partially lost her hearing, for example, she could no longer hear my snoring. And when I lost my taste for alcohol, weed and Pall Malls, she — not to mention my liver and lungs — was grateful.

Losses also can fill our mental safety deposit box of anecdotes. Nancy once got a Jaguar tour of the Civic Center parking lots when she coaxed a young attorney into helping her locate her vanished Camry by pleading, "Pretend I'm your mother."

Then, I confess, there *is* the negative side of the ledger. Topping my list of worrisome recent disappearances is my diminished eyesight, abetted by cataracts. To counteract my growing anxiety, I've stooped to regularly kissing the rings of Kaiser Permanente ophthalmologists and optometrists.

At the bottom of my list of worries are my granddaughter's missing and wiggly baby teeth. I'd be willing to bet the eight-year-old doesn't believe in the Tooth Fairy anymore but firmly believes in each five-dollar bill she gets for slipping a tooth under her pillow.

Lost through inflation along the way has been the value of a buck. I used to give my kids a quarter. And I felt no deprivation whatsoever even though my parents stiffed me completely.

Some losses undeniably are permanent. My underwear somehow evaporated in Europe, for example, while quick drying on a wine-rack. Nancy's luck with AWOL clothing has been infinitely better: A hotel employee once took the trouble to mail her back an unwashed, wrinkled nightgown from a vacation in the Bahamas.

The truth is that my wife rarely frets about losing things. That's mainly because she strongly believes in karma and the fact that she always returns what she finds. I can verify this fantastical account about a wallet she found: When she called the owner to inform her about it, the woman was dining with Nancy's dermatologist.

My wife and I once wrote a song called "Lost It Blues" for our musical revue, *Touching Up the Gray*. Clearly, we're still living out the lyrics despite having composed the piece 16 years ago:

"I've lost two billion pens, three dozen pinky rings
"Over the last 40 or 50 years.
"And where's the car I just parked
"With all its dings.
"I've lost count of what I've lost.
"It's so embarrassing."

But the song ends on a more serious, somewhat melancholy, bittersweet note by referring to what we both consider our biggest loss — our youth:

"Time is irretrievable,
"It is unbelievable
"I had time on my hands,
"But now it's lost."

Finding is, naturally, the flip side of losing.

My 75-year-old wife recently unearthed an old, old, old supposedly lost outfit in the way-back of her closet. She wore it just for giggles while strolling with Kismet one evening. A woman she didn't know approached her just to say, "What a magnificent vintage dress." Without losing a beat, Nancy answered, "Thanks. It goes with the face and body — I'm vintage too."

Getting the hang of living happily ever after

I let the olive oil from the pizza dribble down my knuckles in a cozy suburban New York restaurant. It made her giggle.

Nancy Fox, a blink past 16 that pre-Vietnam winter, was shy. I was, too, so I figured we were perfect for each other.

Within the year, I nervously attached my fraternity pin to her dress, which guaranteed we'd be together forever. Forever lasted until summer when she suggested we "see other people." So, we did. And lost touch. Completely.

Fast-forward almost three decades — past her ex-husband and daughter, past my former wife and two kids. Change the scene to Mill Valley, a small city slightly north of San Francisco. Tucked into a faceless shopping center was a pizzeria. "Woody," she shouted when she noticed me, "is that you in middle-aged makeup?"

Within months, I asked her to marry me. She eventually said yes. But just as we were getting the hang of living happily ever after, the diagnosis was as unsettling as the big Loma Prieta earthquake: Nancy had breast cancer.

Luckily, she survived.

And I have survived being a caregiver, an unfamiliar role for a typical male. While the disease threatened my wife's life, its onslaught, treatments, and aftermath had imperiled my universe.

Today — instead of dealing with surgery, chemotherapy, and radiation — we focus on the pleasures in the mundane life of a *non*-cancer patient and her partner. And every a.m. we make sure to kiss one another and say, "Good morning — I love you."

We bask in the light at the end of the proverbial tunnel. What a relief *that* is.

It's been more than 10 years since the diagnosis, a point that's meaningful for both researchers and statisticians: The odds of Nancy dying from something other than breast cancer have now increased exponentially.

My spouse has become mindful of what she eats and how she exercises. She checks any unusual pains with a physician. She often cheerleads freshly diagnosed females.

I, meanwhile, have been leading a support group for guys. Marin-Man-to-Man.org explains why we meet weekly: The "emphasis is on making…each other feel less isolated, uncertain, misunderstood, or afraid…Through the good times and bad, most men loathe the stepchild-status breast cancer gives them. But the marvelous synergy of our group often acts as an antidote to that particular toxin."

At first, I was petrified the disease would kill my wife. But I've learned, again and again, that a positive attitude can cause a reversal of discontent. I remember, for example, driving to work. A stuck power-company van blocked my way. I fumed about being late. But when I paid the parking lot attendant, who days before said she'd been stricken with ovarian cancer, she changed my grumpiness with one sentence: "I'm happy to be alive."

So is Nancy.

About 250,000 American women, one in eight, are diagnosed with breast cancer annually. That translates roughly into one every two minutes. More than 2 million women in the 50 states live with the chronic disease, but more than 40,000 die of it here each year (370,000 worldwide).

According to the American Cancer Society, 13 percent of U.S. women will get it, with three-quarters of them having no risk factors except being female.

Breast Cancer Awareness Month, a national October phenomenon for a quarter of a century, brings a deluge of memories. I recall, for instance, being forced to grasp in a flash how to be there for my wife no matter what, how to inject humor in our bleakest moments, and how to say "yes, dear" copiously and mean it.

I recollect overcoming my anger at doctors not having instant answers, pharmaceutical companies making life-extending but not necessarily life-saving drugs, and my having no magic wands.

I remember learning what Nancy actually wanted was much more important than what I *thought* she wanted.

My wife has since lived through a melanoma, and I've survived last year's prostate cancer. "We lived through two of yours," I noted. "Now we get to live through one of mine."

We relish that the five-year U.S. breast-cancer survival rate has climbed to nearly 90 percent. And we often think of a friend who's been a professional clown for years. She e-mailed us after the docs found *her* breast cancer. "I feel so blessed," she wrote, "to still be able to make a fool of myself."

To remain sanguine, my wife and I long ago agreed that when minor problems arise — physical, family, financial — we'd say to each other *and* the universe, "It isn't cancer."

Poet Robert Frost once declared that in three words he could "sum up everything I've learned about life: It goes on!"

It certainly does, and despite moments when I'm less than a perfect partner, when I'm relatively selfish or I growl at Nancy, I've never felt so whole. I expect we'll die together in a plane crash in Tibet or some totally unreachable place when I'm 96 and she's only 94.

Meanwhile, each day, each month, each year gets better and better. We grow closer and closer. Our lives are wrapped in bright colors, with more texture.

Death eventually will snag us both. But instead of waiting, we're re-experiencing our fairy tale. One day at a time.

And once again, we're getting the hang of living happily ever after.

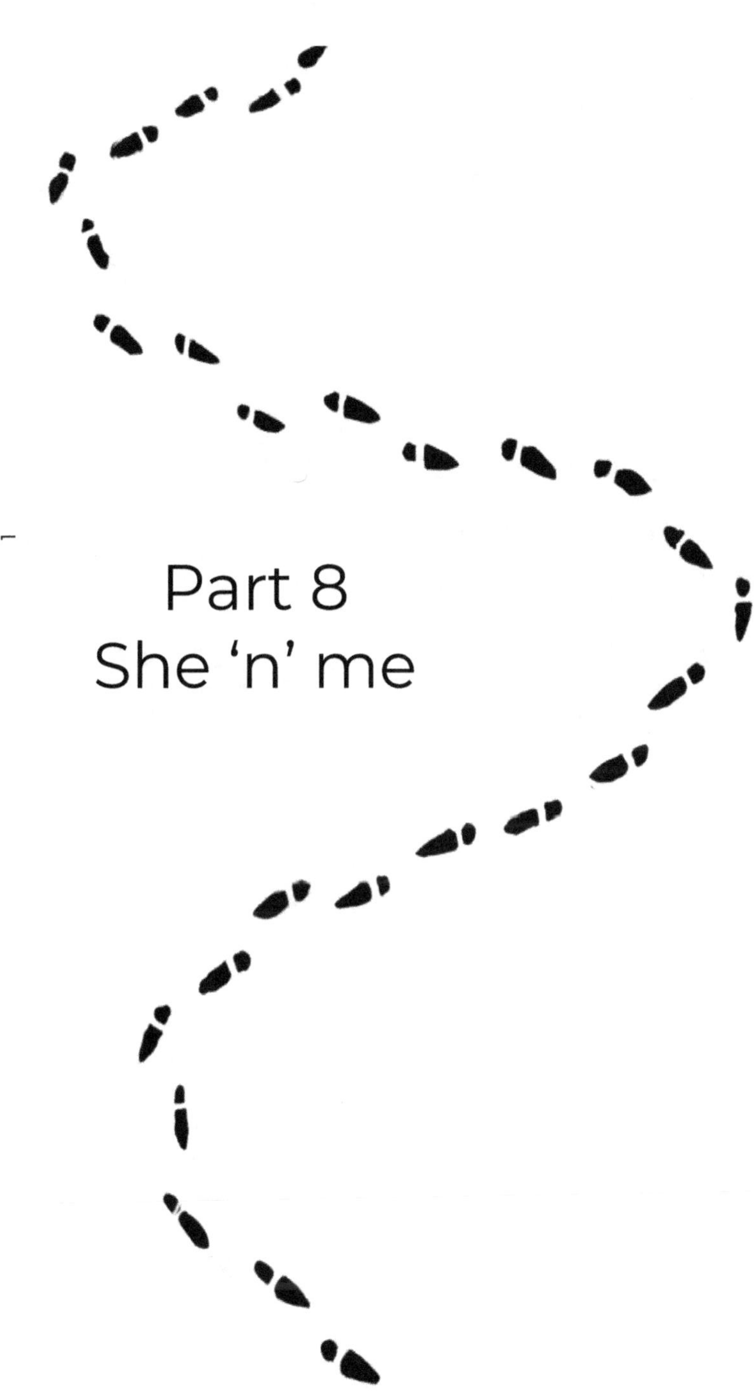

Part 8
She ‘n’ me

Joint sickbed becomes a hotbed for blessings

I used to cringe in disbelief when someone, clearly a weirdo, would swear, “My sickness is a blessing.” Now I’m one of them.

For the second time within months, I was bedridden for a week. Not with anything “serious,” thankfully, but bedridden just the same. A whopping whooping cough/cold/flu/something-else-entirely — maybe the same thing you’ve battled recently — knocked me off my feet. Utterly.

So, I settled in, enduring one coughing fit after another. I rubbed my chest in hopes of jettisoning the burning, and, finally, was able to relax enough to watch the Vinca groundcover grow outside, and my fingernails grow inside.

I happily discovered I hadn’t forgotten how to meditate, and that a flood of good memories from my past incarnations didn’t have to wait until just before I die.

The first bout had been a snap. My wife quickly slipped into the role of caregiver. But this time, a first in our almost 25 years of wedded bliss and jockeying for position, was decidedly different. She violated the First Commandment of our Hallowed Contract of Matrimony: Thou shalt not get sick at the same time thy spouse is incapacitated.

Yeah, we speak like that when we're trying to be clever. Sometimes it even makes us chuckle.

Her symptoms, which replicated but were somehow more severe than my own, didn't make us chuckle at all. And what that meant was, despite my own ailment I had to become an instant caregiver. Feh! Ugh! Perhaps even double-feh or double-ugh!

In the final analysis, however, turning my latest malady into a blessing merely required shifting my perspective a millimeter or two. Instead of whimpering several days in a row that "there's absolutely nothing on TV," I opted to create my own *Law & Order* marathon by switching between two or three basic cable channels. I almost OD'd on it. At least that's what my wife would contend.

Deeper blessings? We listened to music we normally don't have time for, viewed films we'd taped a hundred years back and shoved onto a shelf blanketed with dust-bunnies, and my wife read a Steve Martin novel she'd been hoping to devour eons ago.

Bills and tax forms sat around untouched. Amazing — the world didn't stop spinning on its axis, no collection agencies called, and the IRS didn't use a battering ram on our door.

Our "to-do" list, which never has fewer than 137 items on it, sat idle. So did the junk drawer we'd been planning to clean out.

From our mutual sickbed we got to witness a couple of spectacular sunrises plus an eerie fog cover at the top of a nearby mountain, see a neighbor's energetic Labrador pup bounce across our back yard, and listen to our resident coyotes — which we've dubbed Peter and Wile E., naturally — howl in the middle of the night.

Friends and neighbors, when they found out we were ailing, called with repeated offers to schlep over hot chicken soup or to shop for us. We declined, mainly because our parents, having been children of the Great Depression, had successfully brainwashed us into believing our refrigerators and pantries always had to be overflowing with food. That meant we had plenty of everything needed unless a biblical famine struck.

The sweet, sweet woman next door walked our Golden Retriever, who bonded instantly and couldn't care less that my wife or I weren't toting the leash and the thin plastic bags with which to pick up her poop. We're grateful, of course, that the pooch still has — at almost 16 in dog years — a super-patient bladder and sphincter.

Our respective datebooks became black-lined with cancelled dates.

I couldn't review a couple of shows. I couldn't attend my weekly meeting of the support group I lead for guys whose partners have or had breast cancer or another life-threatening disease. My musician spouse missed a rehearsal for several gigs, a doctor's appointment, and a ukulele-teaching moment. And we both had to skip our monthly film group session.

Somehow, we weathered it all (though we did wish our 5-year-old granddaughter had been visiting since she seems to open childproof medicine-bottle tops a lot more easily than we do).

And we didn't even raise an eyebrow when we had to plow through two glitches. The worst occurred when my mate marinated one of her hearing aids after dunking it in a cup with some un-gulped cough medicine. Second worst was her managing to contract a full-body rash for no apparent reason that required a Rx for prednisone, a steroid that's so troublesome I think even Barry Bonds wouldn't use it.

What made it all worthwhile? Our appetites nosedived, which meant our bodies could each shed a few pounds.

But best of all, the ailment allowed me to weave this column, written, as my sainted late Jewish grandmother might say, so the sickness "shouldn't be a total loss."

Zanzibar?
Staycation features imaginary flight there

We reveled in our fantasy.

Instead of deck-lounging in our Northern California home, our hyper-active minds rocketed us to Zanzibar, the semi-autonomous part of Tanzania in East Africa that's housed humans for 20,000 years.

Why there? God only knows, since neither my wife nor I'd ever before thought of going there, even when playing "let's pretend."

The mental trip was a lot cheaper than real airfare, of course. And we definitely needed a break, fast approaching total pooped-outedness because of our typically intense, neurotic scheduling.

"I haven't spotted a native all day," I mused aloud, "but I have noticed animals nosing around." Three deer-in-residence that devour whatever flowers dare pop up in our yard were grazing only a few feet away. I had no clue what *they* were fantasizing.

Our compulsiveness made us set rules even for the "impromptu" four-day staycation: We'd monitor but not answer phone calls and emails. Nancy wouldn't work on her upcoming piano-and-patter performances, nor I on promoting my book, *Rollercoaster: How a man can survive his partner's breast cancer.*

We mulled taking our dog to a beach, leisurely buying pants at a shopping center, taking out mu shu from a Chinese restaurant.

No deadlines. No schedule. No pressure.

The first morning, I asked our Zanzibarian chef to scramble eggs, with diced onions throughout. When done, I said, "My compliments to the chef." "Thanks," he replied. Funny how much "he" resembled my wife.

The eggs were perfect. But we decided we'd prefer eating out most of the time, as if we were in a faraway Airbnb instead of at home.

Relaxing has never been our long suit, though.

Still, one day we managed to watch a triple-feature in bed. Best of the trio was *Alive Inside*, gifted us by Nancy's cousin, Laura Scott — a documentary about personalized music on iPods breaking through the solitary confinement of nursing home patients with Alzheimer's and other less widespread forms of dementia.

It made us rush to our checkbook.

The film also made me again appreciate Nancy's shows. She regularly plays in memory-care and other senior facilities geographically spread throughout the county. For years she's told me of residents exiting almost catatonic states to tap their toes and fingers, swing their arms, and mouth words from once forgotten tunes.

Our second staycation day included massive laughter and massive weeping at a matinee of the film *The Second Best Exotic Marigold Hotel*, and slowly strolling downtown. That was followed by a day of Nancy dipping into Ann Patchett's anthology, *This Is the Story of a Happy Marriage*, and my reading Roger Ebert's autobiography, *Life Itself*—both with mega-positive messages.

But our best "go-nowhere day" was the one in which we went somewhere. Unscheduled. We rode through manifold tunnels of trees to a nearby beach, where we watched huge waves blithely erase both human and dog prints from the sand for hours. And we topped off the jaunt with an elongated outdoor lunch at a little grocery while watching nearby sheep that were even more tranquil than we. Wristwatches seemed wholly out of place.

Though we did make it through the staycation without working, we also re-discovered our love for — and addiction to — the endeavors that comprise "our revolving-door lives." Well, to be honest, we *almost* made it. Our final staycation hours were corrupted by a computer glitch on my iMac. I gave myself papal dispensation to work it out. Nancy and I tittered at my obsessiveness.

But even if we never repeat our four-day experiment, we at least learned we *can* take time off from overload. Okay, maybe *half* a day next time. Or an hour.

Hey, watch out Zanzibar, here we come again.

I'm a caring husband, but I'm in alien territory

A human foot and ankle contain 33 joints, 26 bones and 100 muscles, tendons, and ligaments working in concert.

Some time ago, my wife's right foot added a sour note to that concert. Two bones started rubbing against each other. Cortisone shots helped for a while. So did special shoes and an orthotic. Ultimately, she needed surgery.

A doctor sliced and diced, inserting two permanent steel screws a month ago. Nancy now can set off airport metal detectors. She chuckles but feels constrained despite having learned to do a sideways cha-cha with a walker. Healing, she says, can't happen soon enough. I agree. I've had to assume an unfamiliar role: 24/7 on-call footservant.

Fifteen steps take us from our downstairs bedroom to our living room. The first day of my spouse's recuperation, my calves insist, I climbed each of them 4,378 times.

I also tripped with a post-dinner tray. Remnants of a tasty beef stroganoff pals had donated scattered like buckshot. Its succulent sauce flew onto walls, railings, and carpet. It didn't match our blue décor one whit. But it did look like a bad Jackson Pollack painting. As I Zouted and scrubbed stains, we rationalized: The carpeting needed cleaning anyway, right?

I worked up to competence.

On the way, I broke a glass and trashed a bagel I'd magically transformed into a petri dish in the fridge.

My kitchen is alien terrain for me — finding a bendable straw is as easy as finding seltzer on Mars. So, friends aided by stuffing our freezer. I'm convinced they run a chicken ranch. The first four dishes we devoured were chicken, chicken, chicken, and chicken soup.

Maybe it's blasphemy, but I've learned to worship our microwave.

My biggest hurdle was fixing Nancy's coffee. I never drink that stuff so didn't know multiple steps were mandatory. First, I had to grind the beans into powder. Steps 2, 3 and 4 involved hunting down an appropriate plastic cone, locating a brown paper filter to insert, and spooning in the requisite milligrams. I then poured boiling water until the drip reached an imaginary three-quarter mark in her favorite mug. Next came the precise amount of Italian vanilla syrup. Finally, foamed milk.

In theory, my wife's battery-powered whatchamacallit spins and creates a tasty white cloud. But I couldn't get it to function. So, she suggested I try another gizmo, a manual plunger. I had to push-and-pull it 50 times. I didn't care: It worked.

All that, of course, was meant to happen simultaneously. Ha!

Eventually I learned. Not one mishap, unless you count when I forgot to put a cup under the coffee drip and, statue-like, watched the counter turn into a coffee lake.

Thank heavens plant-watering takes place only weekly. We have 60 parched green monsters inside, another dozen on our decks. I considered it a triumph that, though several are browner than they were, none died on my watch.

Laundry became another challenge. Although sheets and pillowcases needed changing only once a week, nightgowns, underwear, socks, and shirts reproduced in our hampers like bunnies taking aphrodisiacs. I learned to move everything straight from our bodies to the washer, skipping our hampers entirely.

Also, I can't understand how two seniors, one temporarily incapacitated, can produce enough garbage and recycling to fill the respective containers every 14 minutes.

But Nancy's disability actually let me reorganize a 20-year accumulation under our bed. I discovered what could only be a Dust Bunny farm surrounding a dozen plastic bags crammed with enough flannel sheets for next winter, the one after that, and...into the next millennium, possibly.

Our first post-surgical week consisted of icing my wife's foot to reduce swelling, dumping her bedpan when she had insufficient time to make the bathroom, icing her foot, instructing her about the five remotes we use, icing her, emptying her trashcan, icing her, feeding her painkillers and anti-itch pills.

You get the idea.

Let's say I qualify as a Sherpa, pack animal and live-in valet — or, maybe, a wife.

A friend of Nancy's called, announcing she'd arrive soon to make lunch. "You can do whatever errands you have," she said. "If I don't have anywhere to go," I replied, "will you take care of me, too?"

By Week 2, I'd constructed a routine. I wore my indentured servant status like a comfy old sweatshirt. Exhaustion seemed a perma-part of me.

The surgeon removed my partner's stitches. He said she'd need attention for six weeks more. She wouldn't require a cast. But she'd still need to keep her foot elevated, iced twice daily, with no weight on the toes another month. In short, no pushing the pedal of her car or piano.

Today, she shuffles with a walker. For longer stretches, particularly in the Outside World, she needs me to push the wheelchair. She's definitely improving, though.

I'm overjoyed, but I just don't think I'll be founding a home-care agency very soon.

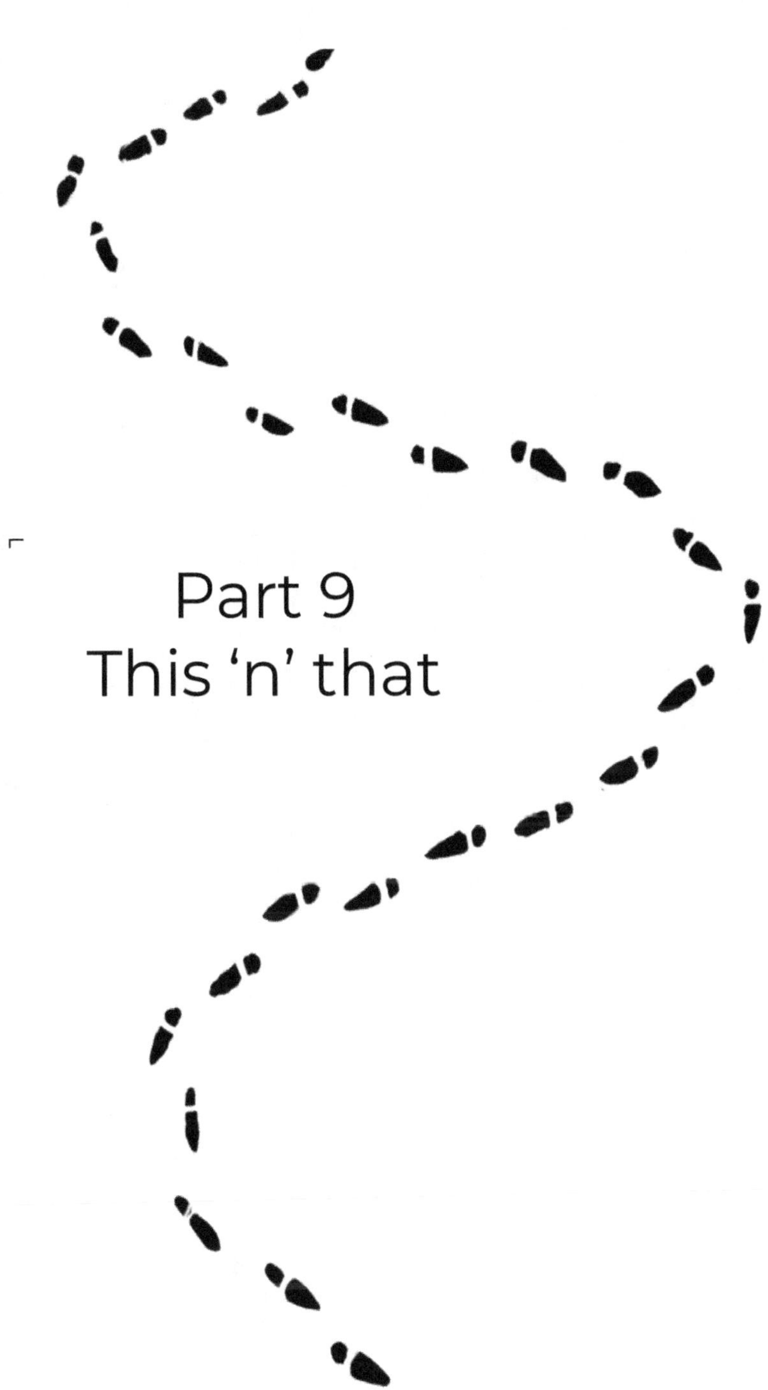

Part 9
This 'n' that

Little Black Book stirs memories of lovers, relocations, true love

I re-discovered my checkered past the other day.

It was hidden — under a stack of less hazardous memorabilia — in a cluttered dresser drawer in the guest room of our home.

The revelations came in the form of a Little Black Book, one of those dog-eared thingies in which wannabe-macho, pseudo-cool guys listed girlfriends and (merely as a mnemonic device, mind you) scribbled how gymnastic their conquests could be.

I used a four-star system.

My wife has always trusted and loved me, thank heavens, so when I told her I'd found a shrieking witness to my chauvinist misbehavior, she shook it off. Mostly. Besides, the book dated back 28 years — to before we were married on the front deck of the century-old former hunting lodge we live in.

And her name, I assured her, was the last one I'd inserted. Because it represented true love.

That particular entry, with letters twice as prominent as most other listings, contained her phone number (underscored three times) and the address of her abode at the time, a place I could live in barely three months before the ghosts of her ex-boyfriends in her bed rattled my cage and amplified my insecurities.

No annotations. No references to her proclivities. No mention of her exceptionally warm and slightly crooked smile, which had captivated me all by itself. Or of how much I loved her then (and, whether she's reading this or not, still do).

The notation did, however, spur an avalanche of memories from the early yo-yo days of our relationship, when we — two only-children — frequently battled for control. We're unequivocally a lot more tolerant of each other now.

I also found entries that might lead someone, erroneously, to believe my main attraction to the opposite gender was to a perky this or a tight that. Those were, the book-directory helped me remember, the misogynistic, pre-AIDS, pre-herpes, sexual revolution days when I could merrily alternate a hot tub romp with a woman that I'd met studying the Course in Miracles with hanky-panky on a houseboat.

In my face, too, popped data for the San Francisco lesbian in a committed relationship I was firmly convinced I could get to switch teams. Defective thinking, for sure.

The book also signaled how my memory's faded: I couldn't recollect entire pages of people. And I found X'd-out addresses where I'd lived in California, Florida, Pennsylvania, New York, and New Jersey. Twenty-nine locations, in fact — including several way stations in Marin County and half a dozen earlier stops in San Francisco. Including tenure at the foot of the University of San Francisco where I lived in a bachelor studio that was bizarrely painted orange and had thick, black bars on the windows.

Including when a female reporter who worked for me on a Florida weekly came to the city to write but chose, instead, to dance erotically at an infamous Mitchell Brothers club. Including an editing phase where a mega-private co-worker mysteriously refused to give her home address or phone number to the weekly newspaper for which we toiled.

Including the remarkable time that a lighthearted friend died of breast cancer in Berkeley a few short weeks before my wife was diagnosed with the disease. Days before my colleague's death, we'd played Scrabble. She put down a word we both knew didn't exist. When I challenged her and reached for the dictionary, she countered, with a massive grin, "Look, fella, I'm dying — I get to cheat if I want to."

Thumbing through the tattered, smeared book, I also found some other non-erotic, mega-cherished reminiscences — a stint in Pennsylvania's Amish country, where my kids were born, for instance. Holy horse-drawn, black buggy — I did relocate soooo frequently. Occupational hazard for a newspaperman, it's been reported.

When I tried to re-connect with some oldies but goodies, just out of curiosity, I found many of the ex-lovers had disappeared into the ozone years before. Maybe Thomas Wolfe was wrong, and I *can* go home again, but the likelihood is that nobody I knew still resides there.

I guess my best — if not sole — option is to live today and every day to the fullest, right here with my loving, devoted wife.

Stupid, klutzy, human – yeah, all those labels fit me

I felt really, really stupid. S-t-o-o-p-i-d.

When the two local firefighters swung by to rescue me, my face turned almost as crimson as their hook-and-ladder. I imagined myself a kitty that had climbed too high in a tree and couldn't get down. But my dilemma was a cat of a different color.

While retrieving the usual scads of ads from our mailbox, which is a block from my San Anselmo abode, I'd locked my Camry keys in the ignition — motor running, pooch whimpering in the rear seat. So, I called 911, and, wielding a Slim Jim and brute strength, my heroes took about nine seconds to get in.

That wasn't my only recent trek into Foolishland.

I dropped notes for this column under my desk and let them sit, not suspecting that our canine might think they smelled tasty. Normally I don't use the "my dog ate my homework" excuse, but I'm invoking it now. Mildly mortifying.

I interviewed my friends. Many asked for anonymity but each grinned like the proverbial Cheshire Cat while regurgitating screw-ups.

One buddy, seeking to be nameless "because I don't want to publicize how humiliated I was," was enjoying a San Francisco Giants home game two rows from the top. When a couple behind him bailed early, he glommed onto the pizza they'd left and started chomping. Oops. He spied them scaling the stairs mere minutes later, and quickly stuffed the box back where he'd "liberated" it.

A friend of a friend reported another food yarn. Attending a San Francisco performance, he was wriggling into his seat when he noticed a familiar face in front of him. His preoccupied pal was unwrapping a candy bar. He decided to say "hi" by silently grabbing the sweet and biting into it. He did. And instantly discovered a case of mistaken identity.

Some storytellers conjure the past. Ed Cushman as a young man, for instance, insisted on testing a chum's belief his tongue could stick to a frozen food container if he licked it. It could.

Etched into the brain of Jack Dawson was a kindergarten teacher who ordered pupils to draw pictures of people. His artistic abilities limited him to stick figures. "To my mind, they looked pretty cool." The teacher disagreed, saying they "should have more 'body' to them." So, he quickly drew a penis "on each of my characters." The teacher's assistant and some classmates "had a great laugh at my expense."

Storyteller mind-burps were rife.

Edward Marson got to a theater and, realizing he'd left the tickets home, pleaded with a box office attendant. You guessed it: deaf ears. My pal had "pinned the tickets to a wall so I wouldn't forget them," he told me just a teeny bit sheepishly.

Another friend must climb 90 steep steps to get to his home. "Three or four times every year," he related, "I get to the bottom and realize I've forgotten my keys."

Accidents also became the crux of many tales.

Gerry Bourguignon remembered working a construction job on Fire Island in New York while in college and absentmindedly driving a tractor filled with building supplies off a dock into the water.

Marv Edelstein reminisced about agreeing to take a female friend for a motorbike ride, then taking off with the disc-lock on. The bike toppled, he and she with it. Though neither was hurt, he said, "she still reminds me of it on a semi-regular basis."

Then there's the one about odoriferous critters.

A female friend informed me of an acquaintance, a guy who lived in a mobile home under which a family of skunks squatted. When he couldn't coax them out, he shot them. But he didn't count on their final act being to let go of an incomparable stink. He couldn't live there anymore. He couldn't find a buyer. He had to sell it as scrap.

Stoopid?

I recently bounced out of bed and, sprinting to the bathroom in the dark, didn't hold my hands in front of me. I smashed into a doorjamb. And whacked my nose. Which swelled. It really didn't need to be bigger.

Should I order my dunce cap now? Nah, I'm just klutzy, perchance ridiculous. Or maybe just human — like the rest of you mortals.

How I overcame a particularly troublesome week

It was, genuinely, the week from hell.

You know the one I mean, when the Dow plummeted more than 1,000 points, just under 6 percent, in a couple of days.

That nose-dive really rattled me because it severely messed with my retirement funds.

Despite that, I'd probably have been okay had I not been surrounded — as if trapped in the eye of a ferocious hurricane — by a plethora of illnesses, emotional predicaments, and other events that caused me no end of worry.

I felt helpless, totally out of control. So, I prayed to a God I tend to believe in only when I'm in deep dung. And, surprisingly quickly, I was able to focus on my own life — and my wife's, and, in fact, my pooch's — being in relatively good shape. So, I decided it was okay to feel okay.

Yes, I do live a happy, Hershey bar-devouring existence, admittedly spent mostly in my home staring at the glare of my iMac screen.

My next-door neighbor/friends weren't doing as well, though.

The guy on my right was suddenly hospitalized with a mysterious leg pain and weakness. Viral infection. In addition, unidentified vegetation was found on his heart valve, so open-heart surgery was momentarily contemplated. On my left, Neighbor No. 2 abruptly became an ER patient in the dark of the night. Diagnosis: internal bleeding. A buddy further away required an eye operation. It went moderately successfully, but he was informed he'd need a series of follow-up procedures, none of them pleasant.

My grandson dropped out of Georgia Tech after less than a week there because he was homesick and desired a "gap year." The Alzheimer's-troubled husband of my wife's friend from kindergarten was put in a locked psych unit after trying to strangle her. My daughter was hospitalized in a New York suburb and erroneously told her kidneys were failing.

Oh, yeah, then there was the petty crap.

My wife caused a minor scratch on a woman's car that cost $900 to fix, and our flat-screen TV fried in a surge (the repairman required $240 to replace the power supply, whatever the heck that is).

Yes, it was the week from hell — uh, heck, for those who find the original phrase offensive. And, yes, indeedy, I did feel a little like the biblical Job. But what all that did, ultimately, was alter my perspective: We're definitely okay and all the others are likely to be okay as soon as the scary stuff melts away.

My bottom line is that I can now more appreciate:

- That I can still pound out reviews and columns on my aging computer even though on rare occasion, to quote Groucho Marx, "I didn't like the play, but then

I saw it under adverse conditions — the curtain was up."

- The frequent 20-minute geezer naps that refresh me.
- Good buddies like 80-year-old Russ Ellis, whose dual exhibit of ink on paper and sculpted found-wood/steel at a local gallery steals my breath away, and Edward Marson, a much younger painter-sculptor at 71 who's getting incredible help — at a nearby art-supply store on the same street — framing his equally incredible montages.
- My wife's tinkling 88 ivories for "the wrinkle circuit" in countless senior facilities within 20 miles.
- A merry memory: My young granddaughter on my slate walkway killing about 417 make-believe flying critters with one queen-sized plastic flyswatter.
- That my wife and I, who've survived three cancers between us, can smoothly live through anything — except, perhaps, old old-age.
- The teeny white rivulets and falls in the waters under a bridge in a downtown creek.
- The fact that I wasn't at Woodstock in 1969, have never been in Times Square on any New Year's Eve, and have no firm idea who was really on the grassy knoll in Dallas. But I did celebrate another birthday last month, and if anyone wants to send me a belated congratulatory e-mail, I'd be thrilled. I'll even make sure to send you a thank-you note.

Duck, parakeets, Schnauzer spur elder-facility joy

It's definitely a cliché: If it looks like a duck, swims like a duck, and quacks like a duck, then it probably *is* a duck.

The first use of that phrase, or at least an approximation, seems to date back to Indiana poet James Whitcomb Riley. But it really didn't matter. Because I immediately recognized the pet mallard at Bello Gardens as — wait for it — a duck.

The domesticated year-old pet is cared for, primarily, by Walter Paredes. The 48-year-old has worked at the assisted living facility in San Anselmo for 16 years. "I do the cooking and a little bit of everything else," he tells me.

Caregiving a duck, I presume, falls into the "everything else" pigeonhole. That includes feeding it rice and veggies.

The duck was brought to Bello by a gardener when it was only four days old. It was supposed to remain only a short time, but, according to Walter, Juanita "just didn't want to leave."

Residents seem overjoyed that she stuck around.

She "was called Juanito for the first week," Walter remembers, "but then we discovered it was a Juanita." She doesn't answer to her name, though — or any other, in fact.

Juanita pretty much has the run of the place and just waddles around, especially when Bello's residents gather in the indoor entertainment center or the outdoor yard. She sleeps in the storage area. Although she doesn't fly much, she does spread her wings getting from that spot to the garden.

She isn't the sole critter at Bello. One resident has a personal cat. But the two pets don't party together. And despite several folks trying to gift Juanita with toys, she's shown no interest, preferring to dip into her wading pool or just sit quietly. If someone tries to grab her, she typically scoots off — as rapidly as if someone had tied a skateboard to her webbed feet. She even runs from Walter when sensing he's about to put her away for the night.

To the best of my knowledge, and that of everyone there, Pine Ridge Care Center in a neighboring town has no ducks. But two resident parakeets do entertain its human residents. "We bring the birds into the activity room and sit them on a table," says Sherry Kass, activities director. "And if there's music on, they sing more."

She contends that although they particularly "have a calming effect on dementia residents," *all* the residents "like to clean their cage." Sometimes, she adds, "they try to whistle the same song the birds are singing."

The elderly residents often ignore the birds' given names, though, and call them by the monikers of pets left behind.

Pine Ridgers also enjoy whatever critters come "to visit any one person, because the pets usually end up playing with all the residents." Sherry says her assistant, Iris Rodriguiz, occasionally adds to the menagerie by bringing in her Chihuahua. "They love Sundae because they can hold her in their laps."

Love Is the Answer (LITA) doesn't have a flock of ducks *or* parakeets. Dogs are another story.

Susan Bulthuis is one of 300 volunteers the nonprofit sends into 38 long-term care facilities in Marin County. Sweet Pea, her five-year-old Schnauzer, accompanies her. "I'm really the chauffeur and Sweet Pea is the volunteer," she tells me on the phone. It's apparent that she's grinning broadly as she says it — and that she's used the line before.

At Villa Marin, which she visits once every week, "Sweet Pea does a high-five and a handshake, and everybody loves it," she says. "She's a show-stopper."

Residents "don't want to let Sweet Pea go," she elaborates. "A lot of them don't get many visitors." So, Susan sometimes stays two or three hours ("although we're only supposed to stay for one"). She visits both the independent living and assisted living sections.

According to Meg Stiefvater, Villa Marin's volunteer director, "residents experience…many losses when moving to a care facility. Providing visits with…pets help reconnect [them] to…pleasant memories while bringing both joy and friendship into their lives."

Nobel Prize-winning French poet Anatole France once determined that "until one has loved an animal, a part of one's soul remains un-awakened." I concur.

I also agree with the motto of LITA, which happens to be celebrating its 40th anniversary: "A little TLC — tender loving care — goes a long way."

Safe from storms,
I bleed for the homeless who aren't

I stayed warm and comfy in my home during last month's over-hyped Rainstorm of the Century and its successor downpours.

No mudslides in my Marin County neighborhood. No trees down. No clogged drains.

I'd joked with friends that, because I live on a hilltop, if my house flooded, I'd start looking for an ark.

Though I'd used the phrase "go with the flow" a shedload of times in the past, the slogan made me downright nervous as the wind-whipped rains approached my San Anselmo hometown each time. So, my wife and I burrowed in. We felt particularly safe because she'd rushed to a supermarket earlier to scoop up five gallons of bottled water just in case our water lines fractured. Or, I guess, if we became dehydrated.

Although we couldn't magically wish away the scary, wailing gusts during that first — beware the oncoming cliché — dark and stormy night, we found more than a little security in cuddling.

But I did have to bail out my hot tub the next day, 73 bucketsful. I'm still not sure how the rainwater kept seeping in and pushing the tub, like the creek downtown, to the brink of its spill point.

All's well that ends well, of course, but I couldn't stop thinking about the hundreds of homeless here. Where, if anywhere, did *they* find refuge?

While I served on the county's 2008-09 civil grand jury, we issued a report titled "Marin's Homeless: The 'Invisible' Problem That Won't Disappear." It recommended, among other things, a permanent shelter. It still hasn't happened.

In the place of action has been lot of official chitchat. Some might label it *bullchit*.

It's clear that the main places the homeless get help, private facilities, can't go it alone. Nor can the faith-based support system REST, a Rotating Emergency Shelter Team able only to put a Band-Aid on a major wound by sheltering some 40 men and 20 women during the worst of winter's wet, chilly, and occasionally freezing nights.

When spring arrives each year, all 60 are dumped back onto the streets to join the ones who hadn't been so lucky in the first place — streets where more than a few have died from hypothermia.

Those tragedies don't make media headlines any more than the people who periodically freeze to death in unheated tenements in Detroit.

It breaks my aching, bleeding heart.

According to the Marin Organizing Committee (MOC), which was formed in 2008 and which has been instrumental in pushing the idea of a permanent shelter, the estimated annual cost of one would be $1.25 million — a sum that could be divided between the county ($500,000), 11 incorporated Marin County communities ($250,000, pro-rated by population); congregations and civic groups ($250,000), and private donations ($250,000).

All the towns and cities except one that's agreed to contribute $16,382 per year have dragged their feet.

Undoubtedly, there still exists — as always — an unhealthy amount of resistance from the NIMBY (Not in My Back Yard) crowds.

So, the homeless problem seems perpetual. On and on and on. As inevitable as winter storms?

Last year, blazes at homeless encampments became an issue when fire departments from two communities had to respond to grass flare-ups. Later, to ward off a likely conflagration, goats were brought to those cities to chomp on dried vegetation. Because we seemingly fret more about property than people (even our most needy citizens), that lame action truly got my goat. It's really no joking matter, though.

What can we — comfortably sheltered residents in a county overflowing with money and a mounting silver tsunami — do? Petition our supervisors and other civic leaders to get off the dime and on the stick.

The grand jury report noted that "unlike the waifs of poverty found in literature and TV dramas, the homeless can look just like an average taxpayer — like an unemployed cousin, a confused mother or father, a fragile grandparent."

It also declared that although "stereotypical images of the chronic homeless suggest ragged people from the lowest socio-economic strata, today's growing rolls include the recently middle class, yanked into homelessness by one unexpected financial crisis or illness.

“To believe we can erase the problem would be naïve, yet to think we can shrink it to a tolerable level is not.”

Let’s.

I peek into a crystal ball and eye being a centenarian

I'm greedy: I want to live until at least 100.

My desire presumes, naturally, that my body won't break down. Or my mind.

But I'm enjoying life too much at 76 to contemplate leaving my home or this planet any time soon.

If I did require a senior facility, I might choose one near my abode so my wife wouldn't need to travel far to visit. But it might not matter since she'd be 98 when I vaulted the century mark and, hopefully, would be nestled right next to me.

She's actually keen on a place in southern Marin County "where the old liberals and hippies, musicians, and other artisans are" — some of them, Seniors for Peace, still protesting outside the facility every Friday.

Hitting 100 doesn't necessarily mean becoming inactive.

Joe Saccone, co-founder of a supermarket chain, was honored recently at a bocce club. That was appropriate because, even at the triple-digit point, he still plays there thrice weekly.

Another impressive local centenarian is Marc Platt, a wrinkle-free resident at a health care center who'd been an original Ballet Russe de Monte Carlo performer.

Platt worked his way through three surnames. He was born Marcel LePlat, gamboled as a Russian-sounding Platoff, then morphed into a modern danseur in the *Seven Brides for Seven Brothers* film, on Broadway in *Oklahoma*, and at Radio City Music Hall as a choreographer.

He remembers dancing at 11 after discovering it'd help him be near pretty girls. He still flirts but can't pursue women quite as easily. His legs don't work well anymore.

His pep, however, is as peppy as ever.

Platt watches "good movies — no junk," checks out the latest cultural morsels on a PBS channel, listens to music ("classical, of course"), and eats heartily ("I like mush in the morning — it keeps me young").

He has no secret of longevity but does tell me, "I take things as they come. I was pretty much always that way."

From bed he greets his daughter with a look of delight, glad for the visit despite her not toting her pet Chihuahua, whom he also adores. "Any day I don't see Donna is a day I'm least happy," he gushes about his adult child. "I love her very, very, very much."

She characterizes her dad as optimistic, straightforward, and stubborn. A perfectionist who's comfortable in his own skin, he interjects: "I'm not easy. I get cranky."

As an avid football fan, he relished the idea of spending Super Bowl Sunday at her nearby place. He's there with some regularity, to lunches, family gatherings, and parties. Because he's 100, however, he does spend chunks of time in yesteryear. Like thinking about being under contract to MGM and the studio forcing him to stop riding his motorbike because of the danger to his legs.

He thinks, too, about Donna's late mom, whom he'd met while they were both appearing in a touring company of *Kiss Me Kate*. And about dancing with his granddaughter, Casey, "in about 5 or 6 *Nutcrackers*."

Regrets? Only one, which he relates with a massive grin: "I had to get over the idea that I can't have sex."

Meanwhile, a Buck Institute for Research on Aging study of worms showed that combining two known systems — the anti-cancer drug rapamycin and an insulin-signaling technique — could extend the invertebrates' life span to a human equivalent of 400 to 500 years.

That sounds too science-fictionish to me. But then, so did the iPod when it first was mentioned.

The term centenarian has existed for more than, coincidentally, 100 years. But elongated life spans have now created a new word, super-centenarian — someone who's lived to 110 or more. It's been predicted the number of centenarians will hit 6 million by 2050, according to the Associated Press.

In 2012, the United Nations estimated there were 316,000 living centenarians worldwide. The U.S. Census in 2010 listed 53,364 in the United States — 82.8 percent of them female.

I thought of those stats as Marc smiled once again and stretched out his arms, inviting me to hug him goodbye. I did. And he hugged back, with more strength than I'd have guessed.

So, I mentally underscored that I want to reach 100. Maybe 110. Or more.

'Hidden' café draws a diverse, cheerful lunch bunch

My wife had to drag me there.

When she first suggested going, my fears of resembling a real old fogy surged like ash from Iceland's Eyjafjallajökull volcano. I would, after all, have to admit that I'm ancient enough to get the entree at the discounted four-buck seniors' price.

But my brow-furrowing was unwarranted — Jackson Café is inviting, buoyant, and a purveyor of scrumptious food.

The eatery is an arm of Whistlestop, a nonprofit that's been lauded for 57 years for providing services to oldsters and folks with disabilities (more than 5,000 annually). Its hidden-in-plain-sight secret is its youthful offspring, the 40-year-old restaurant where everyone's welcome regardless of age or physical condition.

I find it nearly impossible to drive in Marin County for any protracted length of time and not spot a vehicle run by Whistlestop. No wonder: About 50 of them make 400 trips each day of the week, taking folks shopping or to doctor's appointments, spiritual services, or other places they couldn't get to otherwise.

On the other hand, I must have passed the café, perched across from the bus depot in San Rafael, thousands of times without noticing it being there — despite the fact that it feeds 60-80 cheerful people Monday through Friday between 11:30 a.m. and 1:30 p.m.

My wife, who volunteers for Bread & Roses and plays piano at manifold senior facilities in Marin, learned about it from her audiences. "Why don't we try it out?" she proposed one day on a whim.

"We're not needy," I replied, oblivious that I was flaunting my ignorance about its customers. "In no way is that a requisite," she countered.

So, we went, ate heartily, and met Joan Sanders, who easily commutes to the café from her home several towns away. Joan, who'd worked with catering companies and event planners before, carries the title café coordinator. She accepted the post less than a year ago, after volunteering there for the previous four. Her job description? Interviewing would-be volunteers (and ensuring that their backgrounds are checked), training those who make the cut, and deciding which five will act as servers and greeters any given day. "I shuffle them around a lot," she tells me.

Some, she says, "do it to help others, some do it for social contact. Whatever the reason, they work hard, so I make sure they get what they volunteered for."

While calculating who needs to do what, Joan works closely with chef Rocky Packard, who's upgraded the dining room from a cafeteria-like incarnation that featured a single entrée often thawed or dug out of a can. Before he took over, casseroles were a big deal. Now he offers a varied menu with fresh, healthy food: poached salmon, chicken sausage jambalaya, turkey pesto lasagna, beef Stroganoff, and Asian chicken.

On our initial foray, my wife feasted on eggplant parmesan (which came with salad, iced tea, and a hunk of pumpkin pie). I, the ultimate carnivore, went for the more manly basics — a juicy burger and fries.

The volunteers universally seem to love dishing out the cheap thrills dreamt up by Rocky, who started last November after a directorship at the homeless-friendly Homeward Bound. But why did he, a guy with 32 years of high-end restaurant experience on his résumé, choose Jackson Café? "I was tired of the rat race," he explains.

Who's munching on his café creations? An ethnically diverse crowd, including a lunch bunch that hurries over from jobs at nearby offices.

Yvonne Roberts is Whistlestop's development and marketing director. She applauds the rapid changes Rocky has instituted: "He gets only compliments — about the meals, the spices, the complexity of the menus. He even gets handwritten thank-you cards."

Dennis Thompson, who heads Whistlestop's board, is a tad more philosophical. On the agency's website, he writes, "I firmly believe that the spirit and action of volunteerism is what separates the U.S. from most other countries." Volunteers *and* paid staff might all face a big hurdle, however — both Whistlestop and the café could be forced to move if a proposed rail platform literally gets in the way.

For the time being, Joan has taken it in stride. "It's like saying, 'We may have an earthquake,'" she notes, choosing to focus on her day-to-day tasks instead.

Diners have also stayed in the here-and-now. As I eat, I eavesdrop. Three white-haired men each predict the outcome of the day's ballgame. Two middle-aged women chat about a third "who doesn't know the difference between angina and vagina." And a man lunching alone tells a server over and over again how much he enjoys coming there.

Nobody dissents. Not even the once reluctant me.

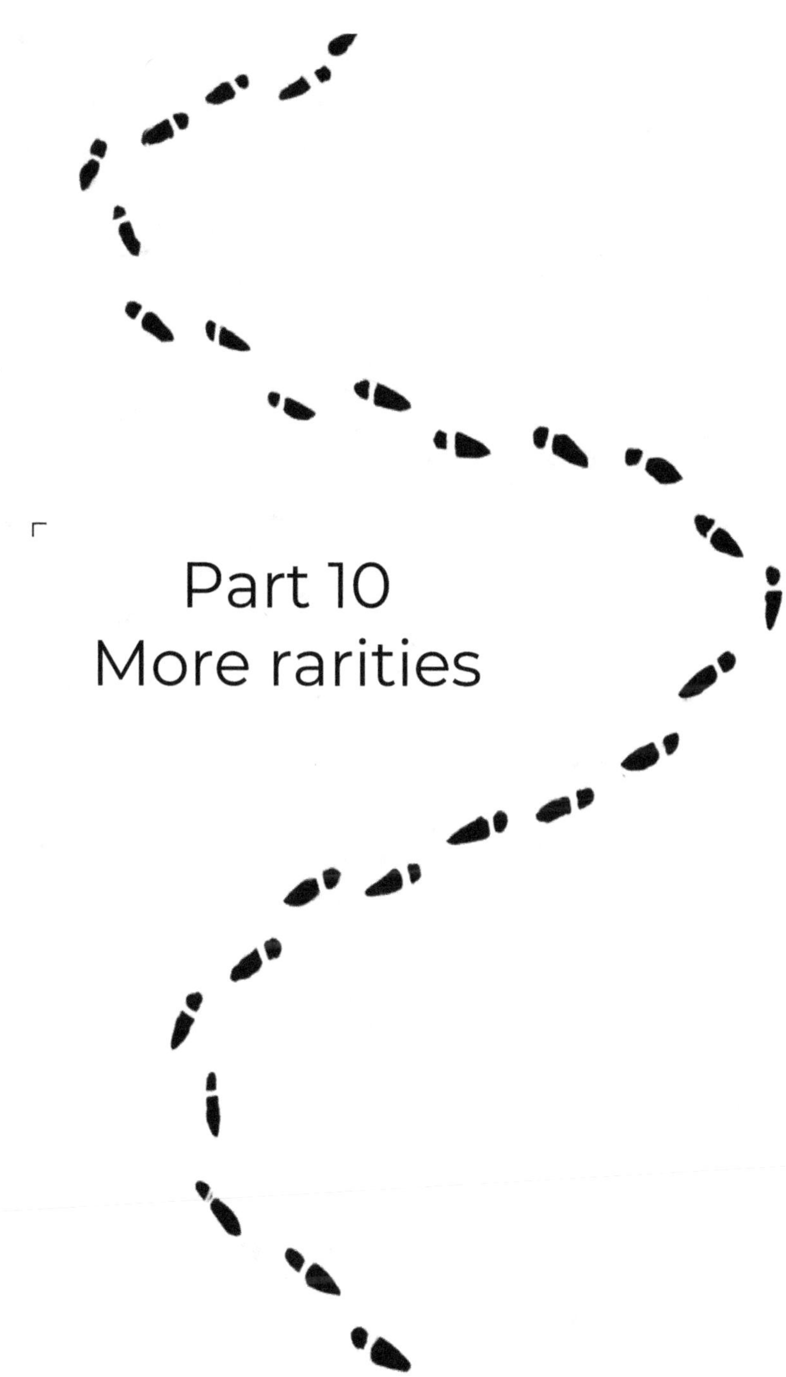

Part 10
More rarities

'Riding shotgun' on a recycling truck can be a delight

Andrew Lendway goes through a pair of sneakers every two months. The wear-and-tear stems from hopping in and out of a $220,000 recycling truck 2,000 times a week.

The Marin Sanitary Service driver picks up six tons of recyclables a day — paper, cardboard, cans, glass, plastic bottles — from three Northern California communities.

Quickly.

His boss, Steve Rosa, thinks Andrew eventually will slow down: "It'll wear him out — that pace is only for younger guys."

At a judicious speed, drivers can work into their late 50s or early 60s. Andrew is now only 33, although his red baseball cap makes him look even younger. His shaved head hides a receding hairline. But he can't mask his energy.

I watch him leap from the truck's cab for 3½ hours without a break. I'd gotten company permission to "ride shotgun" to document recycling efforts. I'd picked his second run, his 4:30 a.m. first one being too early for me to tackle.

Each stop varies. "Some places," Andrew explains, "don't recycle hardly anything; others recycle everything in their house." Occasionally, someone leaves a lone bag with a few newspapers in it. At the other extreme, the muscular 6-foot, 185-pound driver recalls, one family once had 38 buckets lined up.

As we near a home with a large count of bottles outside, he laughs. "Looks like they had a party there."

Large plastic carts from Marin Sanitary, small buckets, and other customer containers — all can reveal a great deal by their contents, in effect "who does what."

In short order I observe Andrew avoid being hit by several drivers who couldn't care less that he's toting plastic carts mid-street. I also watch him back up or pull over to let cars squeeze by ("it's like this all day — worse when school's in").

He croons "good morning" to residents walking their dogs, and chats with locals about "anything and everything." One old woman, he notes, "usually sits in her garage and waits for me. She just likes to talk. I spend a couple of minutes with her but then I've gotta get moving."

Despite the pressure, Andrew, who commutes to the Ross Valley from Modesto, describes himself as "a happy-go-lucky kind of guy."

He wears a soul patch (it used to be a goatee, but he likes to change) and a blissful look. The latter comes from absolutely loving his job ("the only time it's really bad is when it rains — paper and cardboard get soaked, and buckets get filled with water").

He's been doing this route two years and has been "chased around the truck a couple of times by dogs and raccoons."

Maneuvering "tight streets," he tells me, "takes talent."

Andrew keeps in touch with officials via cell phone. But he dislikes wearing the yellow earplugs they supply, despite the regular crashing of bottles and cans on the inside of the truck. And, unlike most drivers, he doesn't don gloves except for "commercial accounts — that stuff can be really dirty." He does, however, sport jeans, a gray and orange-striped company shirt and four tattoos (including one that duplicates a tatt worn by his grandfather, an image copied by his brother and dad as well).

He's a two-coffee-a-day drinker and half-pack of cigarettes guy but indulges in neither the morning I ride. Nor does he snack (I consider that intelligent since the truck lurches each time he pushes the button that locks the brakes, and it shakes sideways as it fills and gets heavier).

Our trip proceeds without incident until the bottom of an ancient container breaks as he lifts it. Bottles and cans scatter. As Andrew hustles to clear the mess, he says that happens more often than he'd like.

Near run's end, he scampers up the side of the truck and jumps up and down to tamp the paper and cardboard so more can fit. I find the action amusing — delightful, in fact.

Andrew finishes up pretty filthy, looking forward to a hot shower and a joyride on his motorbike. I'm still pristine, content remaining a desk jockey.

Marin Sanitary, whose logo proclaims, "Recycling Saves Resources," and its president, Patty Garbarino, are being honored this month by the San Anselmo Chamber of Commerce as business and businessperson of the year.

It's a family industry. Eight Garbarinos work for the company, and that doesn't count in-laws. The family and its Marin Recycling & Resource Recovery subsidiary have spearheaded Marin's 75 percent recycling rate — California's best and 35 percent better than the national average. They were first to institute curbside recycling nationally and opened the initial indoor U.S. dump to recover commercial, construction, and demolition waste.

Andrew believes most people have no idea what he or the company does. "They just see us come by and don't realize it's a lot of labor."

He'll receive no award from the chamber. But he and his 70 fellow drivers do get a symbolic one — from me.

Protester-artist playfully jabs at toxins in society

To say Sierra Salin is unconventional is to state the obvious.

According to a character-reference by Pam Hartwell-Herrero, mayor of Fairfax, it "might be easy to look at him as some sort of wacky, offbeat troublemaker." But that, she says, is because "he challenges the status quo, makes us think about our role in community, and always brings a smile and fresh insight to the dialogue."

He tells me he's primarily a carpenter and artist. But he's also a photographer, jewelry-maker, environmentalist, documentary filmmaker, and playful inventor of words.

Sierra, Pam adds, "is a wonderful family man...ever-present at town gatherings and important meetings. He is a...good person who cares deeply for the planet and all the creatures living on it. He volunteers his time on campaigns that benefit the town."

I find it tough to encapsulate him.

The physical part is easy: He sports shoulder-length, curly dark hair, and a bushy gray beard. A gold tooth shines from the rear of his mouth.

But when he declares "I never grew up," he's not referring to his six-foot stature. It's his man-child passions I can't boil down.

On medical forms, he usually writes, "I am allergic to bureaucracy." He frequently scratches that itch.

The 52-year-old's latest protest targets a 5G tower that would facilitate more cell phones. "Why are we filling the air with electro-smog?" he asks.

His street-theater antics in parades have included a Styrofoam drone augmented by 20-foot high "homeland insecurity" surveillance cameras; a mock nuclear reactor spewing dry-ice radiation fumes; and a "plastic drag," a "visual and visceral" statement about waste and environmental destruction.

When I ask what his first protest was, he friskily replies, "When somebody didn't give me milk."

Interviewing him in his Fairfax back yard, I ascertain he superimposes original thinking on familiar subjects. He created, for instance, a "peace is patriotic" pinball machine for a Marin County Fair.

His environmental focus seems ingrained. He drives his car "as little as possible," opting to ride his bicycle. And he fulminates: "We've got fracking here, Fukushima there, we've got Gulf Oil spills, we've got genetically modified organisms everywhere. I'm really, really distressed about the future."

When he needs to escape, he puts on headphones and stares at stars. "I like solitude and my own space," he tells me.

Outside, he cherishes his gardens and beehives. Inside, he surrounds himself with "external memories." Others might call it flotsam and jetsam.

I'm particularly taken with his wife's weaving-looms and their huge Buddha ("just your basic garage-sale find"). But Sierra is eclectic, unattached to a single dogma. Miniature kitchen flags represent major religions plus Sufi, Gaia, Om, Native Americans.

Fascinating, too, are frames filled with photos of his mother — and her shadow.

His art, scattered, falls into a pigeonhole of "whatever strikes me in the moment."

While comforting, neither artwork nor protests are relaxing. So, he unwinds by singing tenor in a barbershop quartet, and by playing dulcimer and guitar.

He attended two colleges and earned certification as an EMT, which he practiced a long time. But he's most proud that he's "been physically and vocally involved in the schools and my community for years."

He was born Lothar Norber George Salin but toyed with his moniker ever since. He switched to Sierra because he simply adores the land "between Truckee and Whitney." Occasionally he uses Tunafish as a middle name. "People remember it," he declares.

His name-switches occasionally bring trouble — and First Amendment tilting at judicial windmills. Such as a skirmish with El Dorado County traffic officials who cited him for using the pseudonym "Love Heals." Ultimately, he was sentenced to 32 hours of community service.

He once signed checks "Bush Sucks!" — "out of frustration with the state of America and the world." He acknowledges that was "a little confrontational."

He once stood in front of the Good Earth supermarket with a dried-out Christmas tree and sixty $2 bills that he distributed while suggesting passersby "do something for someone else." Many folks, suspicious, ignored him.

He once walked into a police station and said he wanted "to turn myself in because society is a menace to me." "Scram," they said.

When I ask, "How do we change the world?" he responds: "Love each other."

The more he talks, the more I agree. Maybe I'm just a bit wacky, eclectic, and playful, too.

He's collected 75,000 pieces of stuff – a definite 'wow'

Rudy Contratti isn't exactly Peter Pan. He just acts like it from time to time.

Were he 12, you'd expect him to skip a flattened stone across a pond. Or try for a world's record catching lightning bugs. But he's 45.

His age seems irrelevant, though. He's simply a grown-up kid with a contagious spirit and joy of life, an elevated sense of humor, and an uncommon degree of persistence. Plus a love for what he does.

What he does is collect vintage stuff — 75,000 items so far.

Despite that daunting number, Rudy insists he knows "where everything is." To prove it, he reaches behind him without looking and pulls from amidst a thousand things a metal tin circa 1938-41. He hands it to me. "I'm fascinated by how they could imprint the pictures and instructions and colors, considering the technology of the time," he says.

Every piece of his miscellany is placed with artistic sensibility and precision on walls and ceilings and doors and in his front yard in the museum-like home near the sole movie theater in Fairfax.

The ’70s mark the outer limits of Rudy’s collectibles, which start with the mid-1930s. Each of his eight small rooms are devoted to Americana sub-categories, including lunchboxes, ashtrays, hand-puppets, pocket vases, “kissing couples,” lead western figures, rolling pins, guitar picks, small cars and trucks and trains, and “bicycles that fit on the ceiling.”

They’re affixed with staples, nails, screws, glue, and double-sided tape, and each is an original. “There’s no ‘re-pop’ stuff,” he says. “I don’t do reproductions.”

Rudy gave me a jam-packed tour several weeks back. I couldn’t grasp it all, so I requested a second two-hour helping. Both times, it was “a wow!”

My wife had noticed the spectacle first, on one of her dog walks. Instead of white-picket slats, the fences outside are constructed of 130 pairs of skis. Colorful. And offbeat.

The front yard is a fairytale-in-waiting. Odds and ends, more than the eye can capture in a single view. Strangely, everything contrasts and, simultaneously, blends with everything else: A shiny black metal peace symbol constructed from firearms; a gaudy truck front with an Elvis sign; cactuses and succulents and a pampered spiritual garden nook.

But it’s the home’s interior with its endless panoramic montages of memorabilia that is most astonishing. Incredibly, there’s no mess. Why? Because Rudy, whose accent leaves no doubt he’s from New York, tends to be a cleanliness nut.

Employed by Fairfax (“the town custodian,” he tells me), he’s kept the parks, tennis courts, and Little League field “tidy and neat for 22 years.” And he’s been collecting that long, mostly buying — sometimes on extensive “junkin’ trips" across the country. But he's also expert in dumpster diving and accepts freebies.

His fastidiousness extends to non-work hours. If it hadn't, his girlfriend, 37-year-old Shara Randall, might have interceded. "Now he has a professional duster who moved in a year ago — me," notes the woman he's dated five years.

Rudy enjoys the consistency.

From 1979 until singer-songwriter/guitarist Jerry Garcia died in 1995, he was steady in a different way: He chased the Grateful Dead for 300 performances. Like many Deadheads, he occasionally sampled psychedelics. That, he confides, is how he got the vision for his ski-fence.

His bedroom, a flashback to then, features memory-evoking rock 'n' roll artifacts (drumsticks used by Lynyrd Skynyrd, for instance).

The kitchen is a contrast. The couple has stripped it as part of their ongoing process to "clean everything and repaint and redo." Explains Shara, who creates jewelry and works with her family at Reflections, their shop in San Anselmo, the neighboring community. "It's like painting the Golden Gate Bridge. The work never ends. By the time you get done, you have to start all over again."

I can see they're well matched. He confirms it: "It's rare you can meet a girl who likes all this stuff, collects vintage clothes herself, and is able to work an old three-speed pickup."

She elaborates. "We just don't take too much too seriously. And he's the funniest guy I know."

Funny, yes. But definitely a throwback.

Rudy swears he's just "anti-modern." He doesn't like TV ("chewing gum for the mind") or computers ("Big Brother is watching you"). He prefers basking, instead, in what Shara calls "a never-ending art project," what I perceive as a living organism they cull every couple of months.

Rudy also spends time in his outside workshop. There he restores classic bikes, watched over by his other roommates, a bloodhound puppy, and a cat.

In any year, he'll lead 150 people through his home (preferring older folks so his collection can "bring them back to yesteryear"). And every Halloween he opens it to hundreds more, making sure visitors don't think he's selling anything.

"I've had people ask if this is a store. I tell them, 'Hell no. We live here.'"

Four floods and 65 years later, he's still cutting hair

I'm a newbie in San Anselmo; I've lived here only 25 years. Mel the Barber isn't. He's been at the same location since 1945.

How many heads of curly, straight, and balding hair has Mel Bridges groomed in 65 years? "I can't guess," he says. "But I know a lot of 'em are dead." He also knows there's been a vast range, "from two years old to 108."

Almost all were men and boys. "I'm a barber, not a beauty operator," he insists, "though I've done a few women who had short hair."

The 88-year-old chats with me while trimming a fellow who prematurely tries to slip out of the chair. "Wait, don't go yet," Mel implores as sunlight pours through the window and plays off his longish white hair and white mustache. The client slithers back onto the well-worn seat. The barber brushes away loose hair, then uses clippers to even off the neck. Cost: $20.

I ask Mel, who can't remember when he last hiked his fee, what he charged in '45. "A buck."

Now he cuts between 10 and 20 heads a day in his "uniform" — jeans and sneakers. Oscar winner Sean Penn and the creator of the "Tillie the Toiler" comic strip, Russ Westover, have been customers.

Barbers traditionally are schmoozers and storytellers. Mel fits the mold, though he'd swear he's "a listener rather than a talker."

Although his scissors also have tidied many local officials (Councilman Jeff Kroot labels him "a town treasure"), Mel tells me he prefers sidestepping conversations on "politics, religion, and sex." Even so, his customers have figured out he's somewhat on the conservative side. That's why the wife of one regular, Pat Cook, baked him Christmas sweets and, as a gag, signed them Hillary Clinton.

While drawing people from all across the area, Mel says it's local folks like Pat's husband, Steve, who help him thrive. Steve, in fact, relates that last year his six-year-old grandson got his first cut there, and the boy's great-grandfather followed, "a family span of 84 years in just a few weeks."

Mel once employed four barbers, but all passed away. "I can't think of a better reason," he exclaims, "for their not staying with me!"

Antique magazines and random papers jam his chairs. I see little piles, too, on shelving and cabinetry that date back 30 years. Older than the barber himself is a still-functioning 1915 cash register.

Mel once resided in town. He also settled for a while in communities on either side. But for the past 35 years he's been up north, where he keeps four horses ("one's mine, one's my son's, one's my grandson's, and there's one 'extra'"). Photos of him with Arabian steeds he's raised "all my life" decorate his shop's walls.

Mel the Barber, which is how most locals refer to him, says he's a transplanted cowboy from Montana, where he "went to school with more Indians than White kids, and where my granddad lived with the Sioux for several years."

He greatly enjoys speaking about that childhood — and about Coast Guard duty during World War II when he "cut hair after hours." He was prepared for action, on a landing barge, "getting ready to invade Japan, when they dropped the bomb."

In the here-and-now, the tradesman, who acquired two tattoos in the service (one proclaims "Mel," the other "USA"), declares he's glad San Anselmo hasn't installed parking meters downtown: "They'd be bad for business." Robberies would also be bad, but he's not worried — "I'm in a good location, right across from the police station."

Problems? One dry spell hindered his shop in the '60s when guys let their hair grow and grow and grow. And the recent trend toward shaved heads hasn't helped. Nor was Mel thrilled to see his shop flood four times when the nearby creek overflowed.

In each case, though, he simply "opened the door, shoved out the mud, and hosed the place down."

Despite those setbacks, he enjoys cutting hair from 9:30 to 5 Tuesdays through Saturdays. He also loves his time off, including skiing.

I ask about his wife of 66 years, Phyllis. "I better not tell you her age," he says deadpan. Then, after a fleeting pause, wickedly, "She's four years younger than I am."

Mel continues smiling as he offers me a favorite memory: "I began to do this guy's hair and his toupee came off in my hand. It startled me. I ended up trimming around it, but I didn't cut the toupee — it didn't need it, it wasn't going to grow."

Founder of co-op repairs bikes and the environment

I've never seen Jelani Bertoni without his slightly crumpled black hat, indoors or out.

Does he sleep in the fedora, or wear it when he showers?

And his jet-black beard, in youthful fashion, seems a little scruffy — though my suspicion is he purposely trims it to get that look.

Because my own facial hair achieves no level of artistry, and my outfits don't compete one bit with Daniel Craig's dapper attire from his James Bond portrayals, my approach is not to judge a man by beard or lack of sartorial splendor. Especially since I know Jelani's one of the most idealistic, nurturing guys on the planet.

He became founding director of The Bicycle Works, a not-for-profit San Anselmo cooperative that's doing its utmost to pull people from cars and repair the environment this year. But he's no lounge-chair officer. He's also the shop's perpetual-motion chief mechanic and head instructor.

He multi-tasks, for instance, by tilting his head to clench his cellphone so, hands-free, he can give advice while stripping a tire from a wheel.

Visitors to the co-op are greeted by a window display featuring a recumbent bike with a stuffed Curious George as driver. Helmeted, of course.

Bike trappings jam the inside. Tires. Seats. A bulletin-board. Maintenance magazines and books. A 1984 arcade game that focuses on cycling. And, naturally, bikes.

All feed into Jelani's ideals. "This is not just a retail space," he explains. "It's a community-service project, a space where people learn to use their hands to do repairs, to recognize their impact on the environment, and to work together to do tangible things to make the planet better."

My sensation is of witnessing a feel-good family soap opera: An endless line of cheery people stroll in, dodging this bicycle, that accessory.

Co-op membership runs $100 annually — "less," notes the director, "than the cost of one bicycle overhaul."

When it comes to selling, Jelani emphasizes cargo and battery-powered electric bikes. The latter, he insists, "are an important transition technology. People should be doing everything they can to mitigate CO-2 emissions."

His shop, in fact, supplied Marin County "with three non-polluting bicycles to use instead of an ATV or truck." It provided internships for high schoolers and young adults, too, and free services for homeless and low-income folks. Costumed as The Mighty Do-Gooder and sidekicked "by other super-heroes," Jelani also helped deliver 1,200 pounds of edibles to the Marin Food Bank, aided in a creek cleanup, and led a tour of sustainable businesses and farms.

The caped crusader's motto is: "Do as much good as possible while having the most amount of fun."

Jelani hopes to augment his own fun quotient by expanding his space, classes, and staff. For a long time, the

27-year-old was the co-op's only paid employee, but in May he hired a three-day-a-week aide.

He's full-time, unsurprisingly, and so is his consciousness, which stays permanently in simul-tasking mode. He firmly believes that what really "sets us apart here is that you walk in the door, and you'll be handed a tool." Because of that modus operandi, he doesn't think he's competition for other bike shops (half a dozen of them thrive in the area, more than two dozen throughout Marin).

Those who head them tend to agree.

At Caesar's Cyclery in San Anselmo, where Cesar Chang Castillo's been doing business 28 years, the shop owner tells me, "We help schools with safety, free inspections of bikes, and we adjust helmets so they fit perfectly — that makes a big difference in saving lives." He feels no rivalry with Jelani.

At Sunshine Bicycle Center in Fairfax, which has been around since '71, owner Martin Hansen says his shop does "a little bit of it all and was one of the first to start Safe Route programs." The Bicycle Works, he says, is "not really competition, but then, everything takes a little slice of the pie."

The "goal for all of us," Hansen declares, "is that the bicycle movement keep growing."

Working mom wants to run every street in the county

Kira Swaim may not have Obsessive-Compulsive Disorder (OCD) but she's definitely preoccupied. With running.

She's spent five years — so far — running up or down local streets. Several times a week. With no finish line in sight. Her goal is unambiguous: To navigate *every* roadway in Marin County.

The San Anselmo resident prefers paved thoroughfares because the unpaved can be too hard on her fragile knees. And if a street's too steep, the slender, attractive 41-year-old brunette mother of two will walk it. "I run about three-quarters of the time, walk the rest," she tells me.

On those rare occasions when neither is possible, there's always her handy-dandy bicycle.

Her husband, David, 50, originally thought driving every street would be a way to carve out a signature for their then-new business, Tam Realty. The process, he suggested, would let them truly cover all their territory. Kira honed the concept. "By running, we get to know the neighborhoods the way other people don't, to see things you don't see from a car," she tells me while sipping her non-fat morning café au lait from a coffee shop across the street from their office.

Because of orthoscopic surgery, David stopped running. But Kira's still going strong, despite having had "really bad knees my whole life." She's already covered "close to 95 percent of San Anselmo and Fairfax, more than 75 to 80 percent of the entire Ross Valley."

Most of the time, she tells me, she gets a "runner's high."

I remember that sensation from being on the cross-country team in high school, although nowadays I get winded just tying my laces.

Kira confesses that being health conscious and loving natural environs isn't always enough. "One time I went around the lakes and looked for a trail downhill to the parking area after eight or nine miles. My knee had gone out and I couldn't really walk. I asked a hippie lady to drive me back to where my car was. She said yes, but she had to stop at the drycleaner first, then a supermarket."

Luckily, Kira doesn't have to run far to outfit herself. She gets her shoes across the street from her office, where shop owner Charles Yoakum, who once ran for the town high school team, contends he knows local "trails like the back of my feet."

Kira's obsession includes Brokers' Tours days when her peers check out new homes on the market. "The rest are all dressed up," she says, "but I'm not in heels and a three-piece suit — I'm usually in my running outfit."

For a decade, she'd done marketing and public relations for food and beverage corporations but grew weary of 60-hour workweeks. Besides, she and David wanted kids. So, they started their realty office, where they split the workload. She helps clients find the home they want; he emphasizes the final processes. "It's like passing the baton," she observes.

Kira likes swimming and exercising but running is her main thing — dating back to "age 12 or 13, when my parents were starting the process of getting divorced and I took it up as my outlet."

She views it now as "my spiritual time, when I can let everything else go and get a good perspective on my life."

That perspective, of course, leads to the conclusion that not only does she run all over the county, she runs a family and a business. But she believes "it's important to make a clear distinction between our work life and our personal life. Sometimes I just want to be a mom in jeans and a T-shirt."

She loves their daughters, Mina, 6, and Coda, 5, "knowing when I get squirrely and what running does for me. 'You need to go for a run,' they'll tell me."

As for Swaim clients, they, too, can tickle her: She recalls "a woman purchasing a property with a deck 60 feet away from a big tree. She asked, 'Is there any possibility a man could climb that tree and jump into my bedroom?'" David had to assure that buyer the answer was "no."

"I want somebody to produce a reality show that will depict what can come of clients' mouths," says Kira, grinning broadly.

Aging doesn't abrogate work of lawyer who aids underdogs

Carl Shapiro sits in his ergonomic desk chair, the walker behind it a hint his mobility is impaired. He wears hearing aids. But his mouth is not constrained. Nor is his 94-year-old mind.

Quick-witted tales of today and yesteryear fill the compact San Anselmo law office while his hands flail as if intending to put exclamation marks at the end of his sentences. His long gray hair flutters and his bespectacled greenish eyes glow as he passionately talks of defending the underprivileged.

I have trouble getting a word in anywhere despite having been told more than once in my life that I talk too much.

Carl doesn't plan to quit: "Retirement will be involuntary," he says succinctly.

But the former carpenter does look back at his legal career, especially the pro bono segments, with affection. One of his crowning memories is "when I won two death-penalty cases on appeal in one day."

His work — including some on the legendary case of Caryl Chessman, the "Red Light Bandit" who was executed at San Quentin in 1960 — brought plaudits. Mostly.

The University of San Francisco Law School grad has actually filed conventional and clemency appeals for numerous death-row inmates. He's proud of all except one — for Calvin Thomas in 2005. Carl labels it "a charade." Gov. Ronald Reagan had pre-determined to give Thomas clemency, he claims, because the inmate was Black, and the act would be a public-relations coup.

But the Harvard-educated lawyer fondly remembers being "the only one available to defend people for something arising out of political demonstrations." And he smiles when he tells me there was a time the local daily newspaper "wouldn't mention my name because I'd defended strikers. Then they tempered it, but always called me a left-wing attorney."

Carl's been holed up in his office since 1967. The rent, he notes, "is 23 times what it was when I first got here."

He fondles one of the pens in the breast pocket of his tweedy brown jacket as I examine the desk disarray, the framed caricatures, the reminders of his late wife of 65 years, Helen. Carl practiced law with her here, as well as with their daughter, Sylvia. He recalls encouraging Helen at age 57 to enter Golden Gate University Law School, where she graduated in the same class as Sylvia.

For six years, he also partnered in San Francisco with Vincent Hallinan, a Progressive Party candidate for president and a defender of longshoreman Harry Bridges. But he and Hallinan squabbled about Carl's free efforts on behalf of the poor: "One day I went to work, and the locks were changed, so I took the hint and left."

In San Anselmo, he mentored Ford Greene, now mayor, helping him win a California Supreme Court case that let ex-Moonies sue the Unification Church for damages, in effect sanctioning cult-busting.

Carl continues to live in Fairfax with Sylvia, his grandson, and a Chihuahua, in a house he'd bought in 1942 on a street renamed a year ago as Shapiro Lane. "My daughter and two sons are retired," he notes. "Only their father keeps working."

Four years ago, his first-ever accident almost made him quit driving. But he knew his law practice would end if he did, so he's still behind the wheel.

Though he's now rejecting death-row cases (they "take too much" out of him), he remains opposed to the death penalty.

Many attorneys today practice law less idealistically than he has. "Their only purpose seems to be to make money," he tells me.

If his bank account isn't bulging, his memory bank is: "In my first 10 years of practice, I was before the California Supreme Court more than most attorneys appear in their lifetime."

And Carl says he's grateful he can still "go into court and stand up against young people and function quite well."

I'm amused by what he says next: When arguing a case, he envisions "the judges sitting on the toilet — it makes it easy."

Humble he's not. But I *am* impressed when he lists awards he's received (his favorite is from the Marin County Bar Association, for humanitarian service).

The no-longer-youthful attorney is direct. And honest. He'll talk equally about the warts of those he's battled and those he's defended. He's also fiercely opinionated, pulling no punches even when it's someone interviewing him. He immediately corrects me when I squeeze in a personal anecdote about civil rights attorney Bill Kunstler but blow his first name when my memory tricks me.

Carl doesn't worry what anyone thinks of what he thinks — such as his view of the armed man who recently barricaded himself inside a nearby bank branch waving a 17-page anti-capitalism manifesto. He appreciates the guy's beliefs and indicates he might have defended him once upon a time.

I suspect that if he were only several months younger…

Stroke survivor exemplifies courageous, upbeat attitude

Strokes temporarily stole Rita Martin's speech. But it's back, still a bit tentative but good enough so she can be understood easily.

Her courage, on the other hand, never left.

Recovery, she tells me, is "a little, little, little progress at a time. I couldn't talk, and then I could. I was in a wheelchair, and then I was walking."

Rita chuckles a lot, which makes it difficult for me not to adore her. Her overall upbeat attitude makes it impossible. "I laughed in a Tibetan hospital, and in an Indian hospital, after I'd had the strokes," she tells me. "And when I couldn't talk for a year and a half, I laughed."

She labels the date of her strokes, events that occur when blood momentarily stops flowing to the brain, as "stroke-iversaries" — and believes "everyone should celebrate them because they show how much you've done."

I'd first met Rita only a few blocks from my San Anselmo home at a Pine Street Clinic celebration where she'd supplied healthful hors d'oeuvres. Her professional catering efforts, there and elsewhere, are usually gluten-free, sugar-free, and free, in fact, of anything she deems harmful to the body, mind, or spirit.

She tells me she learned culinary arts by watching her grandmother "cook for the whole family, when I was three or four, when she'd make little kids out of challah dough, and I'd put the eyes on them."

Rita also does acupuncture. She's been licensed since 1986, after having apprenticed at Pine Street five years. But she hopes to expand her practice and do more acutonics, needle-less acupuncture with tuning forks.

My wife has been patronizing the clinic for 18 years, adding Chinese herbs to her Western "slash, burn and poison" treatments when first diagnosed with breast cancer. She, too, has a positive attitude. She was never sure what worked — and didn't care. Just as Rita didn't care how hard she'd have to work to heal.

Despite skepticism from a slew of Western docs who thought "I'd never talk and would only be able to watch TV and say yes or no after years of therapy," Rita was certain she could get much better much quicker. She did.

She now sits in my living room sipping green tea. A glamorous 62-year-old, she's clad in the flowing reds and pinks she loves, sporting oversized bracelets and silver earrings shaped like butterflies. It's easy to picture her as a hippie in the '60s. She was just that, of course.

She always liked helping others, even considered becoming a doctor until she realized it "wouldn't be much fun." So, she worked in Albany, New York, for Refer Switchboard, aiding "druggies, runaways, alcoholics, people escaping abusive relationships." Then she helped start the Washington Park Free Medical Clinic there.

She chats now about living on and off in San Anselmo since 1979 — with some elongated trips to Taiwan, India, and Tibet thrown in literally for good health.

Her thought processes sometimes don't make it intact from her brain or heart to her tongue. She doesn't get discouraged though. It wasn't always that way. She "got really angry because the doctors thought I wouldn't get better, and I knew I could. Then, six months into it, I got really depressed."

Usually, however, she'd "be stubborn and figure out how to do it — or think how I could do it differently."

There are "very few things that I can't do now," she says.

She sums up her attitude this way: "Sometimes I feel good, sometimes I backslide, then I feel good again, but all the time I feel like I'm getting better."

And she has no specific advice for other stroke survivors — except that they should "accentuate the positive."

She touts an optimistic book by her friend, Alison Bonds Shapiro, *Healing into Possibility*, and its companion DVD, *What Now?* Alison, who also survived two strokes, says "around 700,000 occur in the United States every year."

Both women emphasize recovery. On the DVD, Rita notes she can hike more than nine miles a day without using a brace or quad cane.

What's ahead? For others, she wants to do "stroke education, where you realize you can get better." For herself, she wants to heal what's still faulty: a right leg that doesn't function fully, a right arm that's flaccid.

And she offers herself the same maxim she'd advise any recovering person: "Believe change is possible."

I'm betting she'll get what she wants — as my wife has.

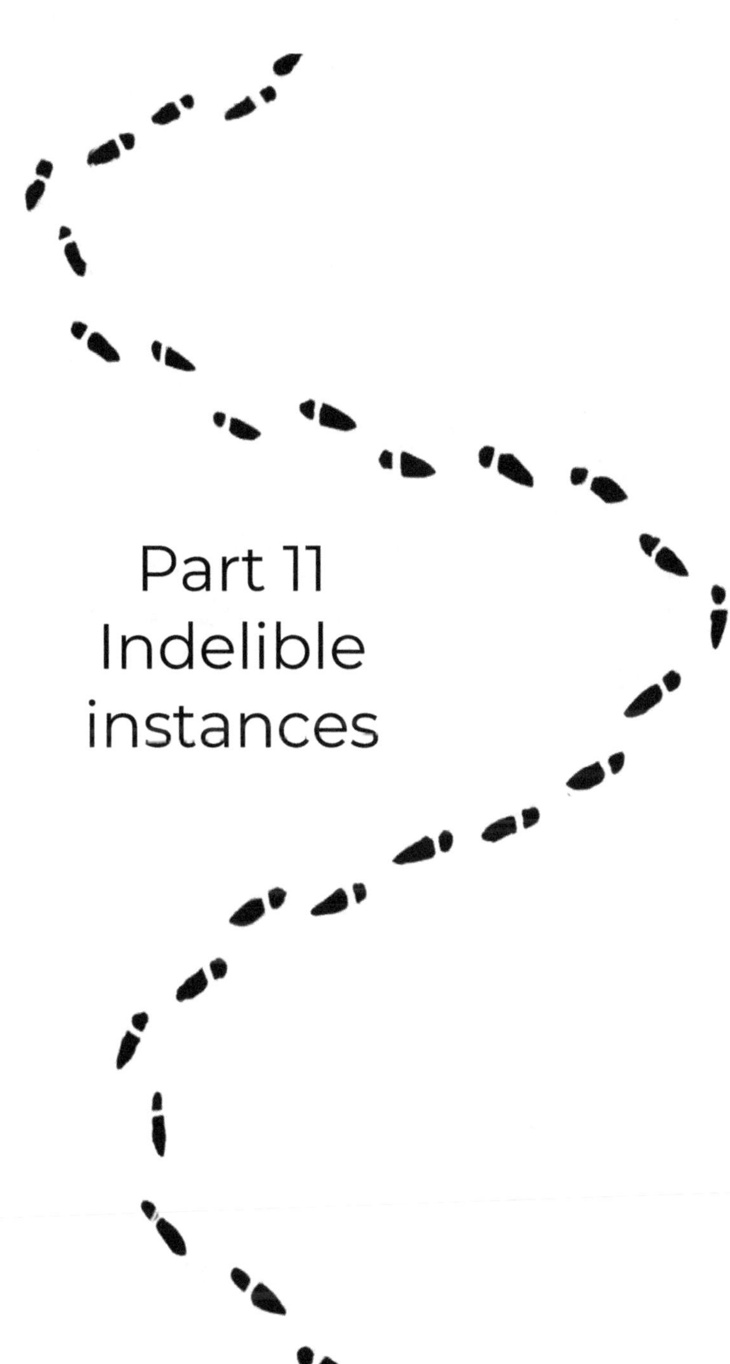

Part 11 Indelible instances

At 75, I wish for everything – except world peace

I remember being 28 years old early last month. But I blinked and now I'm 75.

How in Methuselah's name did that happen?

Walking a tenth of a mile from my mailbox to my home with no breath to spare should tell me my elder status is real. But I still prefer denial.

I'm *on* the hill, not over it, for heaven's sake.

Though no one's dared use such appellations to my face, I can't help recalling a couple of put-downs other golden agers have drawn: Dinosaur. Codger. Nobody, to the best of my knowledge, has ever called me chronologically challenged either, but I think I prefer that antiseptic pigeonhole to fuddy-duddy. It has no sting.

The day I commemorated being alive for three-quarters of a century, my wife and I began it by watching the sunrise from our hot tub. We held hands, just as we had as teenagers. The sweetness was palpable, our joy as enveloping as the 104-degree pulsating waters.

She asked if I had a birthday wish. I thought for a few seconds, then started babbling like the downtown creek on a seriously rainy day. Some of my friends would insist that's nothing new.

My first wish was selfish, that the two of us live until we're 100, in good health physically and mentally. I disregarded the fact that between us we've already survived three cancers, diabetes, hearing and eyesight slippage, more than a touch of arthritis, and skin that looks like Jackson Pollack painted us with a galaxy of liver spots.

A corollary to my first desire was to increase my patience and decrease my temper.

Dream No. 2 was about our kids. I wished my disabled daughter would wrest control of her disorders, her meds, and her life; my son find a new job that brings him success without the stress he's become accustomed to; and my wife's daughter effectively learn to balance motherhood, relationship, and career.

Next up, the next generation. My 25-year-old grandson who's still struggling to find himself lurched first to mind. I wished he could find a stable job, a dependable woman, and much more happiness than he now experiences. For my son's 16-year-old son, a super-duper student, drummer, and artist, I wanted less self-imposed pressure to do well.

Regarding our kindergarten-immersed granddaughter, I wished she could giggle her way through her entire life — and cause all around her to do the same, just as she has in her first five years.

I then expressed the naïve desire, as the presidential race winds down, that both Barack Obama and Mitt Romney stop all personal attacks and run positive campaigns, with that attitude trickling down to political skirmishes across every state, county, and municipality.

Another of my idealistic, bleeding-heart, liberal cravings was that every politician everywhere quit trying to gut the safety nets needed by the needy (especially the homeless, the infirm and elderly, the underprivileged).

My global wish-list was headed by Iran ceasing to develop its nuclear capabilities and Israel halting its threats (and any plans) to bomb that Shia nation. Also, that Israel and the Palestinians find, finally, a two-state solution and peace.

I did think about wishing for world peace but decided it was really, truly, undoubtedly unrealistic (not to mention a teensy-weensy bit overused). So, I didn't. But I did ask that folks all over Earth become more environmentally involved, help clean up shared air and water and, in fact, everything that intrudes on our planet's well being.

My final fantasy was that everyone answers the late Rodney King's "Can we all get along?" plea with a positive shout-out.

As my birthday ended, my wife and I climbed back into the hot tub, held hands again, and expressed deep, enduring love for each other. Twenty-five years and counting for a treasured, devoted marriage. Yes, whatever wishes I made or will make, whether they're fulfilled now or later or never, I firmly believe our love covers everything with several thick layers of okayness.

While cherishing each of my reveries, I recognize what I want most is not to blink tomorrow and discover that I'm 102.

Media disrespect the good work of teenagers

A cadet at the California Fire Explorer Academy couldn't have been more direct. About his 18-year-old leader, Victoria Lis, he said: "I'd trust her with my life."

Trust. Respect. Courtesy.

Those were bywords of the weeklong hands-on training based at Drake High School in San Anselmo.

Working consistently from 5 or 5:30 a.m. till 10 or 10:30 p.m. were 167 wannabe firefighters between the ages of 16 and 18. Plus 104 advisors who'd already achieved professional status.

I interviewed a dozen of the idealists, who came from throughout California and Nevada, finding them roughly 99.2 percent positive. But, as Shakespeare wrote, "Ay, there's the rub." Ask JoAnne Lewis, public information officer for the Ross Valley Fire Department. She can't sell good news to the media because "there's no wow factor, no high drama.'"

She made about 60 fruitless phone calls. Newspapers, magazines, TV, and radio prefer gloom 'n' doom, death 'n' dying.

"If there's a great rescue, or a baby born in the back of an ambulance," it's tough to get into the paper or broadcast, she says. But have somebody maimed or killed in a fire and they're on top of it. Have kids working their tails off at an academy to learn skills needed to save a life, a home, a pet — well, we're sorry, but we have to cover a street protest or shooting or bridge-jumper instead.

I've been a newshound for 50 years and can confirm JoAnne's worst fears: The congregate media motto has long been, "If it bleeds, it leads."

To be fair, most media outlets have been hit with cost-cutting measures that translate into staff layoffs and space limitations. And the academy wasn't totally ignored locally. The local daily ran a few paragraphs and two photos of an abandoned building being intentionally burned. One of six weeklies in a chain ran a rewrite about the same training exercise and a second included a tiny chunk in the town manager's column.

But other on-the-spot coverage? Zilch. Nada. Bupkes.

Vanessa Graves, who hails from Chico, is the academy's food service manager. She's coordinated meals "for eight or nine years." She praises the trainees, who help make lunches and do dishes each night. "It's a lot of work," Graves says about the food prep. "But it's fun." The media is unlikely to focus on that, of course. Not sexy.

Earthquakes. Political corruption. They're much more likely to bring in broadcast advertising or sell papers.

Short-haired cadets wearing sweatshirts with the academy logo or shirts publicizing home posts pass me and ask, "How're you doing sir?" As I chat with Vanessa, I hear, "Thank you, ma'am." The media don't care about politeness either.

Explorers, who are linked with the Boy Scouts, sleep in the Drake gym, their clothing and equipment stuffed beneath cots. The girls sleep separately. But when it comes to training, there's no difference.

Giovanni Montoya, a 19-year-old from Los Angeles, can't pick a favorite activity. "Everything's of interest," he says, "because everything can be used in fire service. I'm a hard-working individual and so are all those around me here, even those who eventually learn they don't want to be firefighters."

He's the guy who'd trust Victoria with his life, even though she's a female, even though she's a year younger.

Some cadets do single out particular exercises they like. They cite "vehicle extrication" or "fire control" or "wildlife protection."

Tuition comes from various sources, with each post making its own rules. Some hold fundraisers to cover the $250 cost (including $50 for insurance). Others foot the bills for their attendees. Some cadets pay out of their own pockets. Regardless, the media don't give a hoot.

Most participants stick it out despite long hours and occasional difficulties. One struggled here with asthma as everything bloomed simultaneously and liberated infinite pollen. Another was extra cautious because she's allergic to peanuts.

This year's 35th annual academy, the first held in Marin County, began with 11 females. Three left. But Sarah Daimantini, 18-year-old from Healdsburg, supplies the rest's perspective. "I want to show up the guys, show 'em I'm not just a weak little girl," she says. "But it's as if they're brothers — they have respect for me, and I have respect for them."

The media apparently disrespects them, however. The lack of coverage proves that.

JoAnne notes that the Ross Valley Explorer post has hired seven firefighters from past academies. They probably don't fret about coverage. Victoria sums up what counts more.

"I liked being forced to get up early, having so much to do, having so many responsibilities — even though it can be really tiring. Last year, my first, I needed two days at the end of the week to recover. You can't come here and just go through the motions."

Somebody, anybody, please alert the media.

Auto-erratic behavior – a what-*not*-to-do list

Shopping for a car can be fun — like having a dentist drill for two hours or trying to find a plumber on a weekend as water backs up from every pipe in your master bathroom.

If you're a fan of dark humor, you might say my adventure started accidentally. With a rear-end collision. In bumper-to-bumper traffic heading from my home toward a state highway.

By trying to avoid the car in front of me that had stopped abruptly, I worsened the impact. The angle caused, among other things, dents in my headlight, hood, fender, and door. No big deal, I figured. One more miscalculation: Turns out that because my Avalon was 14 years old, my insurance company pondered for a micro-micro-second and chose to total it.

"It's strictly an economic decision," the adjuster said when I complained "the engine and transmission are in great shape and there are only 103,000 miles on it and Toyotas last at least 250,000."

Economic decision? Try economic disaster.

The check they mailed was several thousand dollars short of what a decent new used automobile will cost.

So, after we unscrewed my vanity plates, un-Velcroed my

Golden Gate Bridge transponder, and emptied my overstuffed trunk and glove compartment, the search began.

First, rattling around in my wife's 12-year-old Camry, I checked out every parked vehicle I could find in our entire area with a "For Sale" sign taped to its window. Nothing fit the bill.

A late model Prius with every possible accessory was way too expensive. More so the decked-out Lexus. I did locate something in my price range in the next town over — a rusty, dusty truck with an insignia so mangled I couldn't read the brand.

The answer was obvious, painful, and simple: Up our price range.

When I finally managed to calm down from that mental adjustment, my wife and I went to a used car lot a little bit north. What we liked came to $4,000 above even our latest monetary neighborhood.

Then came a Toyota dealership. My spouse acted as advance person, testing a few cars and deciding a hybrid wouldn't work — I don't drive enough miles annually to help the atmosphere much, and recovering the added cost would take from here to eternity.

The "internet sales manager" agreed he'd give us a single price and promised we wouldn't find ourselves in a shootout between salesmen.

On Visit Two to the dealer's lot, we decided quickly that a particular Camry, a few years old, was a good match. The quoted figure was doable. But when we sat inside the showroom, it suddenly jumped almost $1,500? "I made a mistake," the same salesman said.

"But you should honor the price..."

He flashed a paper with the quoted number — along with a list of extras. The total was higher than the new price, which actually was written or typed nowhere.

The dealership's auto game was moving at rocket speed.

In rapid succession, a "team leader," a "sales manager," and a "general manager" apologized but stuck to the higher figure. It was hinted we consider other cars, each a little more expensive than the one before.

"We want the original car at the price originally quoted us." Silence. Even when I said, "Over the years I've found perception can become reality. Were we low-balled? Baited-and-switched? Squeezed by old-fashioned used-car lot tactics?"

So, we left in a huff instead of an automobile, drove home and logged onto Craigslist.

We instantly found tons of choices, the best unfortunately deep into a faraway city. And the owner-seller was a trifle paranoid.

"Fraudulent scammers have e-mailed me, trying to get personal information," he said into his cell. Because of the alleged con men, he insisted on obtaining Google verification of our facts and figures, a certified check, and an agreement to meet him in broad daylight at an intersection of a major public roadway.

In no time he made *me* more paranoid than I'd already been.

We decided to look even further north instead. What we found resembled a real deal from another dealership.

We ended up paying only a thousand bucks over what first was quoted (for an extended warranty that covered the electrical system and some other gizmos we hadn't, naturally, given a second's thought beforehand). But we felt relieved, if somewhat shopworn, and spent about four days basking in our good feelings.

Then came the call.

"We forgot to test everything we gave you a warranty for," a disembodied voice said on the phone. "So, you'll have to bring the car back for a checkup. I know you live an hour away but…"

Almost any day now, with any luck, you may find me showing off my new old Camry.

Counting my lucky stars – and my blessings

Irving Berlin, in '54, wrote a slightly saccharine song called "Count Your Blessings." I've been enumerating mine ever since I first heard it.

Nearly every day I soundlessly list a few things I'm grateful for, borrowing the same notion that Berlin, a Jew, borrowed from an old Christian hymn.

But last month, when my wife and I marked our 25th anniversary, my silence morphed into a flamboyant torrent of adoration: "How do I love thee? Let me count the ways. I love thee to the depth and breadth and height my soul can reach," I recited, brazenly stealing Elizabeth Barrett Browning's sonnet lines from 1850.

Being downright willing and able as a counterfeit poet to gush so transparently, and loudly, is one of my blessings.

I count myself blessed, too, to be a comparatively un-wet resident of a small town well distanced from frankenstorm Sandy and her follow-up squalls.

My daughter, who lives in Yonkers, a suburb of New York City, wasn't so fortunate. She lost electricity and had to endure hurricane winds, thunderbumpers, and blizzard-like snowfalls. But she'd been able to stock up on water and food and candles and scads of pre-crisis sundries before anything happened. So, I couldn't help feeling wonderful when she, a disabled deist who lives alone, told me on the phone, "I'm blessed."

The last few weeks I've also been placing our 13-pound rescue mutt — whom we obtained through a recent Adopt-a-thon at the Marin County Civic Center where 556 animals reportedly were placed in two days — in the blessing category.

He approaches an 11.4 on the cuteness and cuddly scales even though he thinks he's a cat and uses our toilet paper rolls as a scratching post. And since the two-year-old seems to be a wondrous amalgamation of Golden Retriever face, Pomeranian tail, Corgi legs, and heaven knows what else, he refutes the myth that purebreds make the best pets.

He also furthers, in the broadest sense, my fervent advocacy of recycling.

Kismet allows me, too, to derive extra pleasure from quaint but beautiful downtown San Anselmo, where I regularly walk him, and quaint but beautiful downtown Fairfax, where I irregularly walk him, with passersby after passersby greeting us with ear-to-ear grins because of his apparent puppiness.

Truly, he makes me sparkle as frequently as my granddaughter, "Princess Hannah," a marvel on the brink of six and the cusp of perfect.

But putting perfection aside, I also feel blessed that Obama was elected.

I admit I'd often (and nervously) checked Nate Silver's FiveThirtyEight blog in search of hope. I'm truly thrilled I reside in Marin, where a supposedly Kenya-born half-white Muslim socialist who for four years wanted America to collapse could draw 73.9 percent of the vote.

And I'm truly blessed that — although Obama's election truly brought me relief but no elation — Big Bird will survive despite the puppet's existence having been threatened by its creators for a while.

I'm grateful, furthermore, that not everything I'm grateful for is anywhere near Earth-shaking importance. For instance, I love still beating my personal best on Tetris on my beat-up Game Boy.

Being a senior is another blessing. Aging, I find, is an amazing process: As my hearing has decreased, my listening has increased; as my eyesight has blurred, my insights have sharpened.

And despite being certain I'll always adore my wife, who'll forever turn me on, I'm confident I'll evermore find sexy women sexy.

I'm overjoyed I'm in reasonably good health — a few arthritic aches and pains here and there; a few bruises I can't remember initiating; a couple of drippy nostrils.

But I count my lucky stars I'm not the friend who recently rolled from bed to floor and turbo-twisted a leg, another who turned a mountain bike into a weapon of self-destruction and screwed up a different body part, or a third who's recovering from a heart attack.

"There," I reflect in total sincerity if not total belief, "but for the grace of God go I."

A few more blessings come to mind: Being frazzled because our calendar is too crammed with friends and events we simply can't say "no" to, and still having the eyesight, hearing, and buttocks fat to sit comfortably through a play, symphony or whatever.

Best of all, I'm glad I can accept myself — with all my warts — as is.

I love my life, and suspect I could be more blessed, and have more fun, only if I were a canine. To Kismet, every nook and cranny is a playground, everything else a wondrous toy.

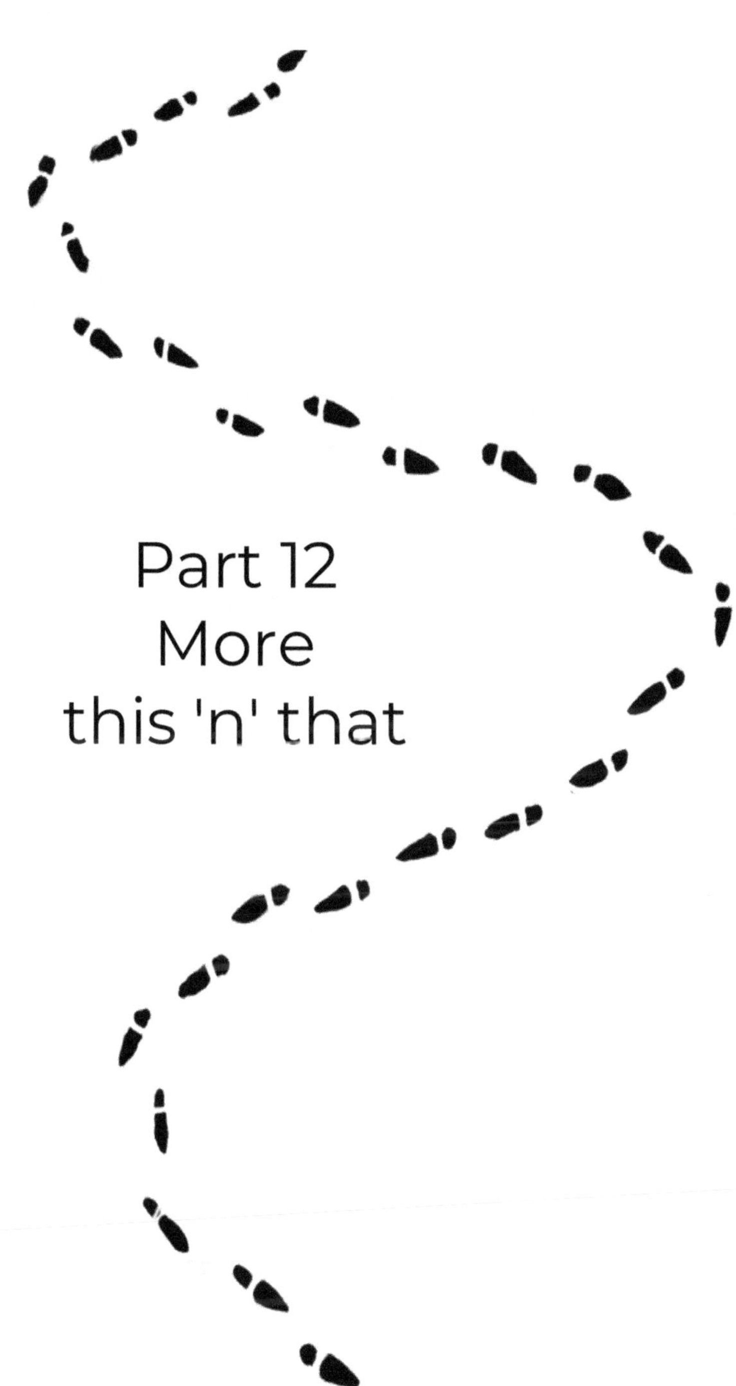

Part 12
More this 'n' that

The verdict's in
– despite imperfections, juries work

Being a juror in an armchair in front of the TV under your own roof is a cinch.

But, as I recently discovered, sitting in a real jury box is a lot harder — especially when, like me, you're a Libra and accustomed to weighing both sides of everything.

I also found that dealing with a real but ordinary defendant up close, as opposed to a celebrity on the boob tube, can trigger sleepless nights.

You be the judge of all that follows in this column.

A federal jury in mid-April deadlocked over whether ex-Giants home run hitter Barry Bonds lied under oath. A mistrial therefore was declared on three perjury counts. Jurors in San Francisco agreed, however, that because he was evasive while testifying, he did obstruct justice — a nebulous charge at best.

The feds originally had wanted to nail him for using steroids, but they couldn't.

Despite some lingering doubts, I think he should have gotten off. Since other Major League Baseball players used performance-enhancing drugs and obviously lied about them, I felt justice wasn't served.

Seven years ago, I waited for a similar verdict.

Martha Stewart, professional purveyor of all things homey and gracious, was found guilty of conspiracy to commit perjury and — here we go again — obstruction of justice. Federal authorities had wanted to nail her for insider stock trading but couldn't.

I disagreed with that eventual decision, too, although my dissent didn't matter one whit. She served five months in prison.

I'd also differed with the jury's decision in 1995 when another superstar, football legend and film actor O.J. Simpson, was acquitted of murder. In that case, I believed the prosecution had fully met its burden of proof.

Early in April, along with 11 others, I helped adjudicate a three-day local trial that triggered questions of ethnic parity, language barriers, and the role of a policeman. After a modicum of impatience and edginess that crept into our opinions on both sides of the deliberations, we ultimately convicted the defendant — a disabled, illiterate Mexican immigrant — of the minor charge of driving without a valid license. But we also ruled that he hadn't supplied the cops with a false birth date. Both were 12-0 votes.

We then declared ourselves "hung" on the third count. The deadlock turned on whether the prosecutor had proven "guilt beyond a reasonable doubt." Five of us had profound qualms. In contrast, a couple of those voting for conviction insisted a unanimous guilty finding should have been "a slam dunk."

Ultimately, a mistrial was declared over the charge that the defendant had delayed or obstructed the cop (there's that vague but useful law-enforcement tool again) or resisted arrest.

Although I'd served a full year on the Marin County Civil Grand Jury, this short criminal trial was much more angst-producing — because we held one man's fate, and possibly his future, in our collective hands.

Had police treated the Latino defendant fairly? The so-called "jury of his peers" — 11 Caucasians and one dark-skinned gentleman — split on the issue. But there was no question the defendant received a fair hearing.

The prosecutor, an assistant district attorney, had built his case on the testimony of the arresting peace officer; the public defender paraded the driver and his family to the stand.

Throughout it all, Superior Court Judge James T. Chou was amazing. He seemed totally evenhanded yet compassionate. His decisions to sustain or overrule objections came lightning quick. His comprehensive charge to the jury was clear, void of legal gobbledygook. And he'd admonish us each time we'd leave the courtroom not to research the case and not to discuss it with other jurors, "friends, relatives, therapists, or spiritual advisers" — in short, anybody.

Just like on television or in the movies.

We heeded the judge's words. During breaks we chatted about movies, yoga, life in the Midwest. Laughter once in a while broke through, like a sunburst on a cloud-filled day. Mostly, however, we remained ultra-serious.

We heard testimony read back, watched police-car videos, and debated points witnesses differed on. As a rule, one person at a time spoke.

Each of us earned our $15-a-day pay.

And I, for one, felt relief at not having been selected from the pool of nearly 200 prospective jurors for the trial next door, which was deep in its seventh week as we began our deliberations.

I also felt good afterwards, when a juror who'd pushed vehemently for a resisting-arrest guilty verdict hugged me.

That action helped me solidify a notion I left the Frank Lloyd Wright-designed county courthouse building with, a belief I hadn't been so sure of before: All things considered, and despite any possible imperfections, the system works.

Buses offer less stress, a bargain, and a chance to snooze

Driving a bus normally induces harmony, but now and then a driver will face a moment of sheer dissonance.

A disheveled musician used his guitar case a little while ago to hammer the bus-door glass when the wheelman wouldn't wait for the guy's lagging buddies to emerge from a music store.

Although I was frozen, alarmed, and paralyzed by the instrumentalist's wrath and loutishness, the driver seems to take it in stride: "I get very few incidents with passengers like this, probably less than one a year," he tells me as he pulls away, noting that he genuinely likes his job.

His resilience, to stretch the musical metaphors beyond where a columnist ought to go, is music to my ears.

I don't take public transportation nearly as often as I should, to be honest, despite concerns about greenhouse gases, climate change, and my carbon footprint. But this particular day I dance to a different drummer (you didn't really expect me to quit while behind, did you?) — I remember to take a $1 bus ride from my homestead to a lunch date a couple of communities east.

The journey makes me ponder why folks who regularly take the bus do. Pondering makes me ask.

Carl Mackie, a sixty-something traveler who commutes to classes, gives me a typical answer: "I just didn't like all the traffic. It's a lot less stressful when you don't have to be behind the wheel. I don't have to worry about road rage or constantly keep an eye out for law enforcement. Besides, driving's too expensive."

Rebel Windom, a mid-30s man who takes Golden Gate Transit to work each day, echoes those thoughts. After finding it necessary to inform me he doesn't "live up to my name — I'm really a gentle guy," he says that for 20 years he's enjoyed seeing "people I know while not worrying about keeping up with gas prices or traffic problems." He also delights in chatting with bus drivers.

I try it.

Wayne Bergstrom's been steering Golden Gate vehicles 17 years. He believes some folks just prefer the door-to-door luxury of their own cars while bus riders squeeze into consistent categories: "Those who are incapacitated, senior citizens, those who've had their license pulled, and those who just like the convenience."

Some also enjoy the coziness — Joan Weinheimer, a 67-year-old sculptor, for example. She became a regular after "20 years of hitchhiking." She loves the seats. "They're really comfy!" she exclaims.

She prefers interacting with others but doesn't get to do that as much as she once did. "People are on cell phones a lot now," she says.

Winter, she adds, has become a bit of an annoyance: "They took the windows out of a bus stop because they didn't want the homeless to use it as a shelter. But when it's really windy or rainy, there's nowhere to stay dry while you're waiting."

Joan has one more complaint: "People smoke in there despite no-smoking signs on nearby poles."

David Rose, a mid-lifer who's been riding buses for about a decade, is one of the few who specifically cite "environmental concerns" as a reason for becoming a regular bus rider.

And Simon Gibbs probably has the most unique motive: The 19-year-old hopes to become a writer and artist. So, although he sometimes gabs with friends when riding together, when alone he asks people if he "can draw them."

Andrew Jordan, 24, does a "reverse commute" busing to work from Oakland — coupled with time on the Bay Area Rapid Transit system. He's not thrilled spending between 90 to 120 minutes on public transportation each day yet does appreciate being able to sleep while traveling.

Somehow, when I finish my commuter interrogations, an anonymously written kiddie song keeps flashing through my brain: "'The wheels on the bus go round and round, round and round, round and round…"

And my musical-pun gland keeps throbbing like crazy. I'll presume, therefore, that even though I may just be preaching to the choir, I shouldn't change my tune after all and, instead, just give you the same old song-and-dance and end on a high note while tooting my own horn.

I didn't really do that in public just now, did I?

Groan!

'Invisible,' jolly custodians keep high school spotless

Sewer inspector. Pig farmer. Garbage collector. Chimney sweep. Hot-tar roofer.

Yuck!

None would ever make my top-five job picks. Nor would scrubbing blood from crime scenes, depicted in the *Sunshine Cleaning* movie.

I'm probably not a high school custodian wannabe either — despite the position being nowhere as distasteful as the others. I am, however, convinced custodians are among the most under-appreciated employees, and must work too hard.

The "invisible" crew of eight as a whole sees it differently, though. In an era when millions keep jobs they dislike because of the economic tailspin, Deborah Ruys, lone woman custodian in the five-high school district, sums up their combined feelings: "I love this job. I love this crew."

It's easy for her to compare: For 20 years she'd run her own housecleaning service.

Robert Amaral, the San Anselmo school's lead custodian, also adores his post. "The best part," he says, "is that we're like a big family. In other areas, administration, teachers, and staff are broken into pieces. Here it's all commingled, and we treat each other as equals. It makes us glad to go to work."

What's the upshot of the lovefest? Well, examine this factoid: If the school's custodians didn't pick up the trash every day, what they'd leave around could fill 300 dumpsters in a year. Imagine the mess that *isn't* there.

I often walk my dog at the school, and almost as often note how squeaky-clean the place is. Litter's almost non-existent. Ditto graffiti.

Yes, a few administrators, parents, and students occasionally offer a thank-you or two, but gratitude is hardly an hourly occurrence. Folks do, however, help make the crew's life painless: "I haven't run into people who don't clean up after our events," notes Deborah. "They're pretty respectful." That's true, she adds, even when "baseball, football, the pool, and gym all are being used at once."

Robert, too, points to harmony. Only once did he need to call in law enforcement — because people lacking a permit became belligerent. More typical — that means cooperative — are meetings like those of Narcotics Anonymous. "You see all those big burly, tattooed Harley riders, the kind of people you'd be scared of if you ran into in a back alley," he says. "But they're actually the nicest people you'll meet."

Deborah, after having subbed three years, is close to finishing the mandatory probation. Next comes permanency, with accompanying bennies and pension.

Robert — who's been at the school seven years, following eight more with the district — says he's especially proud of his jolly night crew, the most invisible of the invisible custodians. "Nobody sees them, but they're here when the rest of us are home with our families."

Walkie-talkie questions interrupt our interview. Robert responds authoritatively yet congenially, a methodology I wish my last boss had mastered. "It's a great way to communicate with each other when we're spread all over and need to ask for help," explains the lead custodian.

"I'm at the beck and call of whatever's going on," he adds, "but our top priority is the safety of the kids."

Cleanliness of grounds and classrooms comes in second. "We'll find everything from condoms to Ziplock bags," Robert says. "You name it, we'll find it." One time or another, the crew has picked up abandoned Christmas trees, old TV sets, ratty sofas.

Graffiti — including chalk outlines of male body parts that found their way onto the football field — has a short lifespan at the school. "The minute we see it," maintains Robert, "we photograph it — so police can see if it links to some done somewhere else — and get rid of it quickly."

This fall, for the first time in years, there's no construction at the site. But now, in addition to caring for older structures and landscaping, he and his crew have responsibility "for the new six-plex, the glass student-center, and the modernized fields."

Robert, who answers directly to the school's assistant principal, periodically returns to the students, whom he contends are everyone's focal point. "I look at it as if I have 1,300 bosses, the kids who go here," he says cheerfully.

When I edited a San Francisco weekly, I claimed 30,000 bosses, equaling our circulation total — but my pronouncement differed from Robert's. I'm positive his positive attitude is more positive than mine was.

Hoping for a permanent job seasonally bell ringing

I don't believe in Santa Claus — not even when John Toomey, a Kris Kringle look-alike, assumes the role. But I do believe in bell ringers for The Salvation Army.

Let me elaborate.

Macy's in San Francisco fired John, who'd been their Father Christmas for 20 years, for telling "naughty" jokes. An elderly couple had complained. One line that drew condemnation was that it was "too bad" the couple had been good all year. A second was that Santa was jolly because he knew "where all the naughty girls and boys" lived.

I consider both double entendres (which he'd been spouting for years) harmless. And I call Macy's puritanical. Prudes, however, seem to believe the gags deserve another kind of gag.

Bigwigs at Lefty O'Doul's, a hofbrau near the department store, didn't think so. They hired the sacked Santa to front an annual toy drive. He also landed a momentary gig on *The Tonight Show* with Jay Leno. Being canned had obviously led him to 15 minutes of fame.

I have no problem with that.

Sadly, other bell ringers employed strictly for the Christmas season have received no attention.

I do have a problem with that.

Irrefutably, none of those stationed in Marin County this year have resembled the traditional St. Nick (except for their floppy red-and-white caps with bunny-tail décor). Sure, they had red kettles and red aprons. But none had white beards or grandpa glasses. None were fat.

Several, in fact, were women — and African American. According to Emily Jones, envoy at the agency's headquarters, ringers also were Latino, Asian and Haitian.

The 31 hires get paid minimum wage. But that doesn't stifle their enthusiasm, whether they stay in one spot or are rotated. Not hitting the agency's $75,000 goal can't turn them off either, because enough has been collected to provide holiday food, clothes, and toys to a bunch of needy families.

Nathan Wallace rings outside a supermarket. It's his first crack at it, and he tells me it's "going good." He'd prefer steady work, though, as a landscaper or warehouse stocker.

Mitch Pulver jingles outside a Salvation Army Thrift Store. Another first-timer, he created a routine. "I like to ask people what the greatest nation is," he informs me. "And then I say, a dough-nation to the Salvation Army. Or I'll say, what is the best city, and I answer, genero-city." People "with kids seem to give the most," he adds. "And those who give seem to be happier than those who don't."

He hopes to find "steady employment in construction or retail" post-season.

Outside a different supermarket, Gwenetta Davis sits on a bench. The agency allows her that luxury because she suffers from spinal problems. "A few minutes ago," she says,

"I got a big ole check for $1,000. The guy wanted a tax receipt, so I gave him our headquarters number, but I got to say, 'God bless you.'"

Two of her daughters are also bell-ringers — Mercedes Morgan, outside a drugstore in the same center, and Shauntrese Richardson, at a second drugstore across the roadway. When the holidays end, Gwenetta says, she intends to return to classes at a community college.

Both daughters, however, want full-time employment. Mercedes had been working for a web designer but was laid off just before she applied to the charity. This job, she explains, gives her "a chance to give back, because when my lights went out a couple of years ago, The Salvation Army came with hot water, soup, cots, and emergency aid."

Gary Peppers is ringing outside the Post Office when I saunter up. "I generally say 'Merry Christmas' to people," he replies to the question kindled by John Toomey's firing, "but they let us say whatever we want as long as it's respectful and comes from inside."

He quit a janitorial job to become a bell ringer but was glad to do it because it gives him, too, "a chance to give back." He says he hoped to find permanent work with ceramic tiles or in a showroom afterwards.

The Salvation Army's ringing actually started in San Francisco in 1891, when a captain decided to use a crab pot to collect money to feed the homeless.

Emily's pleased to inform me that two ringers have found permanent work early this year with stores they were stationed at in 2009. This season, the jury's still out. She hopes, of course, that bell ringers looking for permanent work will find it. If she had to pick only one person to help, though, it would be "Norman Bos, a mentally challenged man who's been ringing at a Post Office for three years. He's a neat guy, and his attitude and heart are so pure, we wish we could clone him."

Maybe Santa Claus will belatedly bring *him* a non-seasonal job.

The village that aids older adults can do almost anything

No, nein, nyet, I refuse to surrender to the oldening process.

I totally reject the idea of becoming as wrinkled as a Shar Pei and spending my twilight years switching back and forth between re-runs of *Jeopardy* and *Wheel of Fortune.* Instead, I plan to maintain a feverish pace into my late 90s and only then — maybe, just maybe — watch Vanna White flip vowels from her walker.

I'm lucky. I've collected enough friends, relatives, and colleagues to act as a support system/safety-net/social-grid that keeps me honest. And I belong to a neighborhood association that shares names and numbers of plumbers, electricians, weed-pullers, and you-name-its.

But I know plenty of folks who aren't that fortunate, people who could benefit from a mindful coterie. Yes, Hillary Rodham Clinton may have borrowed the notion from an African proverb, but she was correct: It often does take a village.

Voila! Consider the Ross Valley Village, a networking group for seniors. The main aim of this new community organization is to help people remain in their homes "with grace, confidence, and peace of mind." That's not to say convalescent centers or other senior facilities in Marin

County don't do a competent job, but this group's organizers think many do better in their own environments.

Barbara McDonald, 73, one of three steering committee co-chairs, tells me the organization fills gaps by "feeding minds, bodies, and spirits." It may do that by directing oldsters to exercise or photography classes, book or knitting groups, walking, or dancing ensembles, or by finding chess- or online chat–mates.

Village people — a small army of volunteers, not escapees from the campy 1970s pop group — also might locate professionals or volunteers who'll provide rides to medical appointments or grocery stores, help pay bills or repair a chandelier, or assist with yard work, pet care, or errands. In addition, the group may make referrals to agencies and service providers, obtain discounts (not only for "early-bird specials") or facilitate the making of new friends.

But "one size does not fit all," emphasizes the website of Marin Village, the parent organization.

Paula McNally, another co-chair, tells me the Ross Valley contingent will develop according to the needs of its members but will use another group that formed a year ago as a template. The 71-year-old thinks social connections are a key element "because isolation can be depressing. I know people who have moved to senior homes only because they don't want to be alone."

Memberships in the village, not limited by age, cost $200 per household a year. But the fee's tax-deductible.

Recent activities have included yoga classes, a restaurant outing, a brown-bag lunch, and forays into San Francisco to see *Tales of the City* and twin museum exhibits about poet

Gertrude Stein. An improv acting class and one focusing on art (from Impressionism to modernism) are ahead.

The village concept stemmed from a 2006-07 Marin Civil Grand Jury report predicting a tidal wave of aging heading for the county. One of every three residents is expected to be 65 or older by 2030. Loulie H. Sutro, a 76-year-old who sat on that jury, read a story about Beacon Hill Village, a seniors' organization in Boston. She flew there to check it out, then started a task force that led to Marin Village's incorporation. She's its board president.

Help with transportation, she says, is the prime need, "but what people ask for is all over the place, like handyman services and removal of couches." The oddest request she's heard about came in Boston, where a "guy who couldn't drive wanted someone to take him to the dog races. Somebody did."

The local villages, she believes, can be "a good friend." Members "can ask anything and we'll try to do it," Sutro notes. "I don't think people are used to that."

Ergo, with apologies to Karl Marx, I herewith prod Ross Valley geezers to "Unite — you have nothing to lose but your boredom or isolation."

And here's a pop quiz: How many seniors does it take to screw in a light bulb? Answer: None, if they get help.

Is art whatever you foist on an unsuspecting public?

"When I was a student," long-time community college teacher Chester Arnold tells me, "The definition of art was: 'Anything you can get away with.'"

Perhaps, he muses, it still is.

I'm interviewing him after a satirical film titled *(Untitled)* propelled my mouth, brain, and belly into laughing-out-loud spasms.

I'd watched it in a local art-movie house, where it screened for about a day and a half before vanishing into a big movie archive in the sky. "Satire," according to the late playwright George S. Kaufman, "is what closes on Saturday night." Here, box-office death can happen even faster.

But I — and the few others who'd ventured into the classy local Art Deco theater — loved seeing the film deflate the pretentiousness of art-dealers, devotees, avant-garde musicians, and on-and-off-the-wall painters.

It did so in one scene by focusing on a white pushpin in a white wall. Installation art?

Kicking a metal bucket — that's music?

Uproarious.

In the '70s, I'd brush-stroked acrylics onto canvas but hadn't stuck with it long enough to get ego-involved. Some paintbrush-wielders I knew didn't escape the trap, though.

Chester is more charitable toward radical art than I. Although he believes "anything that can't survive satire can't justify its existence," he also thinks "there is value in everything if you look at it with a generous perspective." Artists, he says, must "continuously try to redefine the parameters" — even if dullards like me can't grok their motives.

Lake Hanyu, owner of a local gallery that nourishes artists, looks at the issue through a multi-faceted prism. She, too, paints. "Art," she says, "is expansive, always moving. It can convey messages, be therapy, share what the artist is feeling, or stir emotions." Modern art, she reasons, is all about communication. She equates it to both cave paintings and talk shows. But defining it is problematic, she says, because "it's completely personal."

Some art is pure gimmickry, Lake concedes. "And there's good art and bad art, for sure — but who's to say which is which?"

Jo Smith, director of a Society of Artists gallery, suggests juried shows can help assure quality. "I laugh at a lot of stuff that some people call art," she confesses, "but everybody has a different idea of what it is." Art, in her opinion, "is anything that's in the brain."

John Pusch, co-owner of yet another local gallery, concurs. "You can call anything art — it's all very subjective, and all open to question. But the idea behind fine art is that it generally requires high levels of skill."

Fake art may be another pitfall, however.

I recently re-viewed *F for Fake*, a cinematic Orson Welles portrait of a world-class art forger. The mockumentary also dissects author Clifford Irving, whose legacy to the Art of the Bogus is having written a so-called autobiography of recluse multi-millionaire Howard Hughes. The film brings up a crucial question: Can a fake be so good that — especially after experts authenticate it — it becomes real?

Just last month a suburban Chicagoan pleaded guilty to selling counterfeit prints of Picasso, Dali, Miro, Chagall, and Lichtenstein on eBay. Decades ago, I bought a Dali print and wondered if its "certificate of authenticity" was authentic. I also questioned if a lithograph could truly be "original art."

So, what *does* constitute art? I'd visited the Guggenheim Museum in New York City years ago, shortly after it opened. At the foot of a spiral staircase inside the building by Frank Lloyd Wright, a hunk of something-or-other glared at me. The naked chrome car bumper stood tall, attached vertically to a black stone base. Nothing had been added or subtracted. No design was etched into the surface. No spots or lines embellished its shiny face. No chips marred the metal. No strings or tags dangled. The title didn't help. "Car bumper," the label silently screamed at me.

"The art world's gone bonkers," I wanted to yell back. I didn't.

Recently, several installations at San Francisco's Museum of Modern Art outraged me with their presumption that I, the viewer, was brain-dead. One was a randomized pile of stones. Another exhibit featured a musical composition without notes.

A brilliant sequence in Lily Tomlin's one-woman play, *The Search for Intelligent Life in the Universe*, spotlighted the comic-actress trying to show aliens the difference between a can of Campbell's soup and an Andy Warhol rendition. "Soup," she labeled the first. "Art" she called the other. Then, by shuffling them behind her back, she indicated they were interchangeable.

Sure, most art is legitimate, created by inspired people whose true wage scale might average 17 cents an hour. Yet there's a tiny percentage that's simply garbage. Maybe I should amend Chester's tongue-in-cheek definition just a bit: *For a few charlatans*, art is anything you can get away with.

Those who are helping homeless youth need our help

Think ambassadors and you probably conjure an image of gray-haired white guys in black tuxedos. I want to change that concept.

Picture, instead, invisibilized teens and youths who resemble the kids on your block. But these are homeless, often hopeless, and need help. That's where Ambassadors of Hope and Opportunity steps in.

Zara Babitzke, a midlife social worker who'd been homeless several years herself, founded the agency. She'd worked with troubled teens a while, but her program was cut when funding lapsed. Zara found that she couldn't walk away from youths who needed to trust someone, that she "couldn't be another adult in their life who would abandon them." So, she gave birth in 2005 to AHO, a nonprofit with 24 community partners.

"Fifty-five percent of our referrals," she assures me, "are youth referring other youth who often don't feel safe and don't trust the Establishment."

Brittney McDonald is 18 and heading for the University of California at Berkeley via scholarships. She'd finally located a safe place to live after three years of "couch surfing" (staying in other people's apartments). But, to break from an environment "where drugs, sex, and even murder were a part of everyday life," she had to work three jobs simultaneously.

Brittney's now part of the 25-member AHO Youth Task Force, composed mainly of youth who've been homeless or at risk.

James Hayes is 25. He's a Brazil native abandoned at birth, dumped into an orphanage where he was abused, and adopted into an American family at age 10. But that didn't work out either. He ended up homeless for more than four years. He now has a two-year-old son with his girlfriend. He's received financial aid, he informs me, and plans to return to school full-time.

Jimmy was instrumental in organizing Youth Connect, a recent one-stop event at a center for homeless 16 to 25. There, 60 young host-greeters helped guide visitors to stations where they could get tips on shelter, employment, food and clothing, or medical, mental health, and legal support.

I wanted to see it first-hand.

A sign leapt out. It listed celebrities who'd been homeless, including David Letterman, Jim Carrey, Kelsey Grammer, and William Shatner. I also witnessed more enthusiasm and energy than the Project Homeless Connect adult versions upon which the event was patterned.

It drew 87 teens and young adults, 33 of whom subsequently were placed in jobs. Twenty found housing. But that's only a drop in the reservoir. More than 600 local youth still stay with friends or sleep in cars or in the hills. Many of them have been abandoned, abused, neglected, or banished from their homes.

Jordan Atkinson, 20-year-old couch surfer, was there. He's been homeless on and off since 2006, when his divorced father's businesses "fell apart because of the recession." He showed up because he had a broken finger and no insurance. Through the event, he obtained medical attention. "Overall, it was unbelievably helpful," he says. "I was escorted to every single booth that could help me. I even left with a job interview."

Help in some cases means keeping youth out of jail. Last year, almost 2,000 18- to 25-year-olds were booked into the county cells — at an annual cost of, reports indicate, $40,000 per inmate.

In contrast, AHO's total shoestring budget last year was $45,000. Even at that level, though, the economic downturn has put the organization on the endangered species list.

Some see Vince Chew, 20, as AHO's poster boy. He's won civic awards for his work with youth. He holds an office job and takes community college classes. He stays with a friend and hopes to attend the University of California at Irvine soon. He wants to become an attorney.

His back-story, though, is chilling.

He'd been homeless in New York and California, was a drug dealer in the former, and hung out with gangs because he "was paranoid in the streets." He did time at the Riker's Island prison and watched nine friends die within five months. AHO, says Vince, "gave me help when I needed it real fast."

The Ambassadors organization actually has aided more than 700 homeless youth, but last month was forced to send out an urgent plea for funds. It has enough, says Zara, to stay in business only through the summer.

Readers can help by supporting AHO's upcoming fund-raising car wash.

I, for one, believe my affluent county can't let an organization that promotes "giving a hand-up, not a hand-out" fold. So, I urge you to send it a donation. I'm mailing a check as soon as I'm done typing.

Breast cancer awareness should transcend pink ribbons

This month is *not* National Breast Cancer Awareness Month. October was. So that means we needn't think about it for the other 11 months, right?

Certainly, every American woman who's had the disease — all 250,000 diagnosed annually, all 2 million living with it — can relax because it'll automatically go into remission until next October. No?

Maybe that's why I'm angry.

Despite claims that October's pink-ribbon barrage will fill research coffers, I don't think awareness should be limited to one month-long streak of sentience a year.

I live with a fabulous woman who contracted breast cancer 20 years ago. Yes, she's survived the disease, the treatments, the trauma, and the aftermath. But my wife's survival doesn't for a minute mean she won't shudder the next time she goes for a mammogram. Or every time she feels a twang in her right breast. Or the other one. Or, indeed, each time she gets any kind of ache anywhere.

I'm outraged because I know breast cancer is chronic and can recur *anytime* and, therefore, I must spread hope 365 days a year.

The truth is that breast cancer hasn't quite cornered the U.S. market on October awareness. That month also has been abducted by advocates of sudden infant death and Down syndromes, infertility, pizza and liver and popcorn, domestic violence, dental hygiene, LGBT history, blindness, cyber security, mental illness, Hispanics, and Americans with German, Filipino, Italian, and Polish backgrounds. Not to mention dwarfism. All of which seems to spread awareness a little thin, I contend.

I'm livid that pink ribbons — whose main goal initially was to fund research for a cure — have become a marketing tool for all sorts of merchandise that have little to do with breast cancer and a lot to do with profit.

Do I worry about potential repercussions of making my resentments public? No, especially since I've published a book with a VitalityPress imprint that not only chronicles the downs but the many, many ups of my being a caregiver for my wife. I'm hoping it will appropriately distribute awareness.

Rollercoaster: How a man can survive his partner's breast cancer is available at bookstores and through Amazon. It can help if you want to learn what you might go through as caregiver or patient, what advances have occurred in breast cancer research and medicine, or where to find help. My book's aimed at men, but I firmly believe women — especially patients — can definitely benefit from reading it.

But you know about us guys — most believe we can fix *anything*. We can't. Most loathe being vulnerable. But we must be. And most despise surrendering control. Yet sometimes we're given no choice, like when our partners get a life-threatening disease.

For 19 years I've been running Marin Man to Man, a weekly support group where drop-in members often decode what physicians and other healers say (or don't). Along the way I've picked up a few to-do's. I share them in *Rollercoaster*.

- The physical and mental health of a male caregiver is as urgent as those of the patient.
- It feels good to let go of anger at doctors for not having instant answers; at pharmaceutical companies for manufacturing life-extending but not necessarily life-saving drugs; at yourself for not having a magic wand.
- It's crucial to remember each person is an individual, not a statistic (and that breast cancer couldn't care less about race, creed, sexual orientation, or politics, that it's the most common cancer among Israelis *and* Palestinians living in Gaza and the West Bank).
- Downloading or renting comedies, taking walks, reading, or listening to whatever brings you pleasure, encircling yourselves with folks who evoke positive feelings — all may boost your spirits (and your partner's).
- Living one day at a time is good medicine, but best of all might be doing today what you've postponed forever.

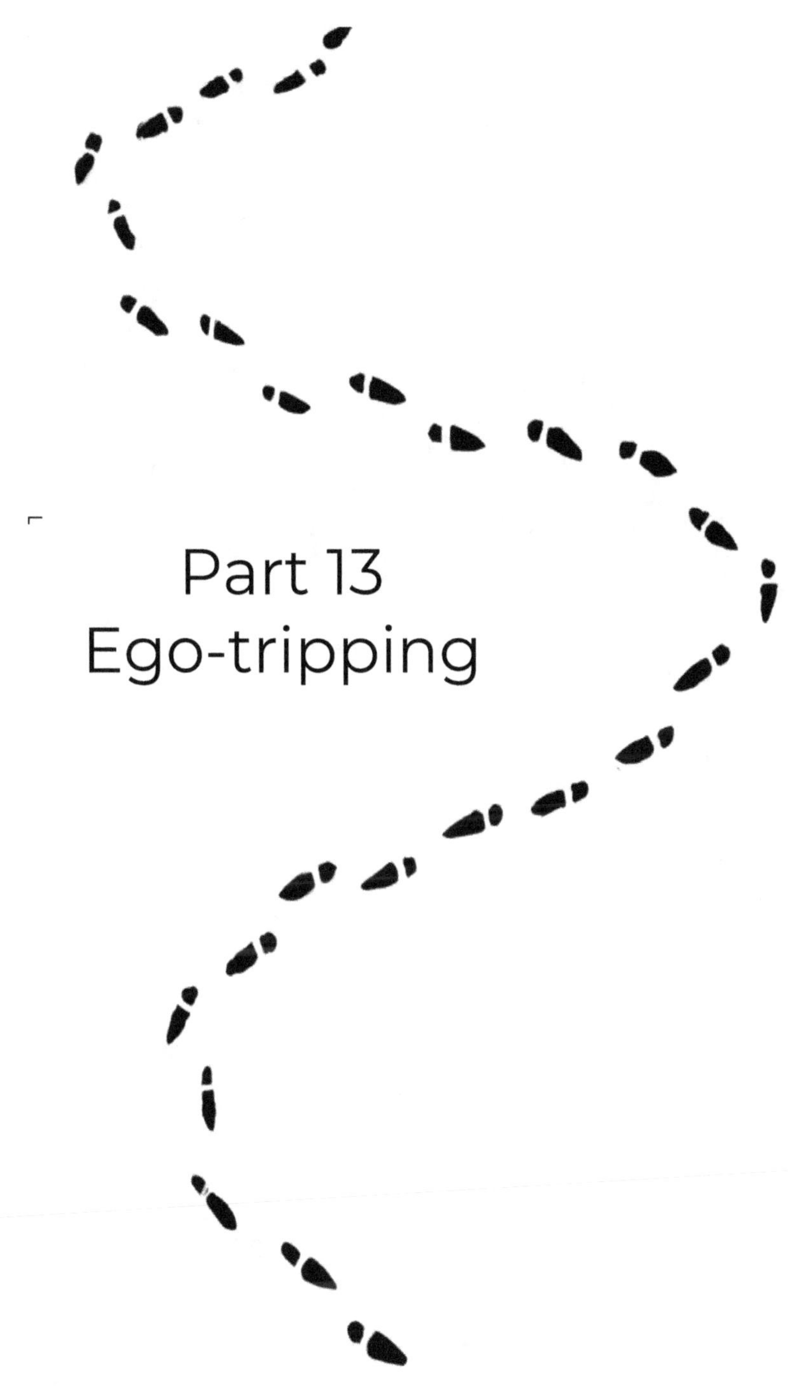

Part 13
Ego-tripping

Is my entire life just one big gamble?

I'd lay 9 to 5 odds that my wife, who comes close to zero tolerance in such matters, is 100 percent positive I'm a compulsive gambler.

Maybe she's right.

I'm ashamed to admit that for years I futilely bet with what she'd most likely call "reckless abandon." Yep, I'd buy *two* $1 Lotto tickets at a local convenience store nearly every week.

If you really need to know, I blame my mom for the nasty habit. She once said, "Sooner or later, *somebody* has to win The Big One."

But on my luckiest lottery day ever, I walked away with $7.

Having had the good fortune to figure out, at last, that a 1 in 40-million probability probably doesn't work in my favor, I quit. So, California's educational coffers now come up short a couple of bucks with regularity. Hey, don't knock it — the way the state budget's been going, that *could* make a difference.

I likewise confess, as a token of good faith and full disclosure, that I'd earlier been addicted to driving *annually* either to Tahoe or Reno for an overnight gaming binge. I'd go with a pal who has since traded views of the Golden Gate Bridge for the boonies. We'd hike a little, gobble down a pound or three of gooey buffet carbs, and then sit hour after hour at the penny slots. If our one-armed bandits got benevolent and spit out several hundred copper-plated zinc coins for our oversized cups, we'd wildly raise the stakes and hit the nickel machines.

My buddy usually ended up dead broke. That meant he'd lost five bucks (maybe 10 in a particularly flush year). I, on the other hand, would methodically scope out each green felt cover in search of a hot table, then irresponsibly toss my small "entertainment allowance" at a blackjack dealer or craps croupier. I'd usually break even, but in some years would accumulate a small tower or two of a casino's chips.

The problem was that my spouse could never accept that I'd beaten the house.

Her point of view was uncomplicated, as transparent as fresh rainwater streaming off a mountain not far from our home: I deserved, at least, to suffer prickly pangs of guilt for my wayward ways. Being a winner simply didn't match that criterion.

I think she thought the serial numbers on the bills that stank from communal cigarette smoke all started with 666 or had been fouled by the ghost of "Bugsy" Siegel. Clearly my winnings consisted of — on every level — "dirty money."

Ergo, desirous of retaining a happy home, I went cold turkey.

I've never actually pictured myself as a gambler — despite investing in stocks as the market dropped like a hot-air balloon with a gigantic leak, brilliantly starting up a losing business in mid-recession, leaving fresh fruit on a car seat in 95-degree heat, and buying a fashionable jacket destined to go out of style in the following half hour.

Mark me misguided, perhaps, but give me a break: No gambling labels, please.

No tip sheets for the ponies pile up on my desk. No Bingo daubers hide in corners of my drawers. I barely know what March Madness *is*, much less understand which teams to scribble into the brackets.

I won't deny that I — heeding advice from *Consumer Reports* — don't buy extended warranties, thereby courageously daring mechanical objects to fail. And as mental images of dime-ante poker-playing undergraduate days ooze back, I'll come clean about a few topical transgressions:

Yes, I've wanted to stroll into a local shoppe to try chocolate-covered grasshopper ice cream — a true gambling rush. I've driven past two schools smack dab in the middle of morning drive-time student drop-off jams. Dicey behavior? You bet. And sitting on a bench, I've pondered starting a conversation with a complete stranger. Well, that surely could be hazardous to my well-being.

I've sat through a screening of *Sex and the City* at a movie emporium, one of six guys at the chick-flick surrounded by 122 women. Was that chancy for my alpha-dog/testosterone street cred? And I've even frolicked alongside my dog right by the kiddie playground in a local park. Obviously, a gambol — oops, sorry, wrong word.

Worst of all, I recently participated in another lottery, one for the 2008-2009 Marin County Civil Grand Jury. My name, along with 15 others, was pulled out of a drum. Randomly. Winning lets me to serve for a full year with no guarantee I can make a difference. Yet another gamble, come to think of it.

Maybe I really *should* ask my intelligent, understanding, compassionate and politically correct wife if she knows when Gamblers Anonymous meets next.

Ego-tripping leaves zero time for 'retirement'

In the latest chapter of the serio-comic novel that makes up my life, nothing fits my comfort zone better than the old chestnut of giving back.

A year ago, I was "let go," and immediately got nervous about what to do with all the "extra time" I'd have. No longer would I be a full-time journalist who got off shedding light on the underbelly of everything and occasionally trying to save the world. For the first time, I'd be a homebody.

But most people would agree that where I love living just isn't that exciting. And I knew that if I simply hung out at the local dessert shoppe, I'd wander downtown streets each day hauling 350 floppy, superfluous pounds around.

My wife seemed even more worried than I: Because I'd scampered past the unofficial retirement age and wasn't exactly the best prospect for a paying job (there's no Walmart in the county so even being a greeter was out), she was sure I'd be uncomfortably underfoot all the time.

I visualized being squooshed beneath her size 9½ Double A's with regularity.

But was she, a part-time public relations consultant, also skittish about my learning how she'd spent *her* extra time for the last couple of decades? Would I discover she'd sneaked in unauthorized naps after chopping jicama for midday salads?

Nope and nope.

My wife, as all who know her know, is nobody's dummy. She let me detect for myself that new activity gobbles up extra time like a voracious Pac Man from the Good Old Days.

Besides, she knew it would take no time whatsoever before I got antsy and had to do *something* to keep from going bonkers.

Writing this column was one of my first outlets — it helped give my "life of leisure" a hint of structure. It does take time, believe it or don't, to think up what to write about. Ten or 15 seconds at least. Then, after I've rejected an initial brilliant idea, and probably a dozen more, I come up with one that might really work.

Next, it takes quite a few more ticks of the clock to interview subjects or visit local sites I'm going to illustrate. The biggest chunk of time, however, is always reserved for the writing itself. Re-writing, actually; then re-writing several more times — all the while pretending it's a breeze instead of an exercise in bloodletting.

The Roving I, it turns out, was just the beginning of constructing something more — a complex structure that keeps me busier than when I was gainfully employed, a structure that lets me give back and ego-trip at the same time.

For the past six months I've been a card-carrying Marin County Civil Grand Jury member. We're investigating all sorts of fascinating stuff, and will be for another half year, but if I revealed any of it, I'd be subject to a jail term. For real. Keeping our actions and deliberations secret, that's what the penal code demands.

I also spearhead a weekly support group for guys whose wives or girlfriends have, or had, breast cancer. I can't say much about that either. We've also pledged confidentiality.

In both situations, I struggle with the constraints. Ask any of my friends: Keeping my mouth shut isn't something I do easily.

I can happily disclose, however, that I also hand out monthly awards at local council meetings. As chair of my community's sustainability commission, I get a chance to give back by honoring those who, each in their own way, give back, too.

"Unsung heroes" who've received the environmentally focused Green Award during its first year of existence include a guy who led between 10 and 15 creek cleanups; a female who marked her 18th birthday with friends by clearing French broom from a lake area; and an architect who designed and built a park, saving it "from being an asphalt jungle."

And the broader Silver Award has featured an 85-year-old who pushed for rehabbing public tennis courts; and an artist who restored the metallic deer outside Town Hall and directed a tile-and-mural project at another park.

All make a difference locally.

In case you were wondering, I'm not expert enough to quash the rift between Jennifer Aniston and Angelina Jolie. And I certainly can't end hostilities between Israel and Hamas permanently — maybe one reason Barack Obama just became president rather than yours truly. But I do think I can continue to give back, one small piece at a time, not unlike the many who participated in the recent national Community Service Day.

And maybe, just maybe, I can stay out of my wife's way. And live out the housewives' mantra about retirement that marriage is "for better or worse, but not for lunch."

My scaredy-cat fears: big cougars, little bugs

I'll cop to it — cats frighten me. Oversized wild ones, that is, especially when they're prowling in my 'hood.

I'm talking about cougars here, the four-legged kind, not the older-woman breed that's been gaining in popularity.

There have been a dozen sightings in my area the last six months, including a pair on my street, where several deer apparently became a midnight snack. Reports of a cougar (aka puma, aka mountain lion) near my home, which borders on open space and a forest, un-dammed my adrenalin. They made me concoct a worst-pun, worst-case scenario: The puma family that preys together stays together.

They made me feline, too: a scaredy-cat.

I absolutely recognize the actual chances of my being mauled are as remote as my being run over by a clown from Cirque du Soleil in a Model-T. Therefore, my fears are way out of whack (particularly since the number of sightings purportedly isn't any greater than previous years).

I also understand that if I do make eye contact, I'm not supposed to run but "make myself big," wave my arms like a banshee, make noise, and throw rocks — if I happen to be carrying one in my pocket. That may be thc ideal prescription for safety, but what if the cougar hasn't read my local police department pamphlets detailing how it's supposed to react to my reaction?

Zara McDonald, exec director of the Felidae Conservation Fund who spoke at a recent community meeting, believes "public education is absolutely essential to help people overcome their fear of pumas."

What, however, if my mind refuses to be educated?

Local red-flag news reports (decidedly more un-soothing than online articles warning about bed-bug infestations prior to my recent visit to the East Coast) may have washed my brain. I have no doubt whatsoever that they've once again turned me into a worry-wart — a frequent emotional legacy from my mom.

Although I need to dispel rumors that the furrows on my brow grow an eighth of an inch deeper every half hour, I nevertheless can't keep the critters, which I'm told can grow to 200 pounds, out of my cerebral cortex. That kind of weight would constitute one mammoth pussycat, one lacking the mischievous charm of Garfield, wouldn't it?

Anyway, because of all the trendy vampire movies, books, and articles around, my mind has even meandered into darker terrain: I've fantasized that not only are those creatures roaming the hills, at least one of them is a werepussy.

I tried, as a defensive measure, to ward off evil spirits one bedtime by cataloguing (in alphabetical order, of course) related terms for my condition: alarm, anxiety, apprehension, disquiet, dread, foreboding, misgivings, nervousness, panic, trepidation, unease — plus my all-time favorites, "the willies" and "the creeps."

Creating the list didn't ward off a thing.

So, after fretting momentarily about a neighbor's black kitty that likes to use my back yard as a litter box, I started playing with a few new thought-balloons. Which, in turn, morphed into another list.

Here, then, is a hint of what's caused me to shake 'n' quake a little bit lately:

- Like billions of others, I mask my fear of flying, especially while being squashed in a seat in an airborne tin can. Yet I accept as gospel the concept that if God had wanted me to soar, He'd have provided me with feathery wings — or at least a flying Batmobile.
- Considering the excessive peer pressure on young kids nowadays, I'm troubled by the notion that my three-year-old granddaughter may start insisting soon that she wants to pierce this and tattoo that.
- A bicycle thief is on the rampage locally. I'm afraid I need to lock up my bike. Oh, wait, I forgot: I don't own one anymore.
- I'm troubled by the idea I might die in 30 years without having watched a single reality TV show.
- Having zero desire to activate an avalanche of animal news, I still feel compelled to report that a downtown shop posted a window sign announcing the theft of a giant toy bear worth $800. Hey, do I need to lock up all my stuffed animals now?
- I've pondered — in a real nail-biter — the impending end of the Earth. After all, it's only half a billion years or so away, scientists report.
- Oh, my, sightings of a black bear were reported at the tail of last month to seashore staff about 18 miles away. We've been told there's nothing to worry about, that at the first smell of humans, the bear — a scaredy-

cat of sorts itself — would wander off harmlessly. I can barely contain my relief.

Do-Nothing Day
turns into a full-fledged fiasco

My entire life, even as a toddler, I've felt a compulsive need to be productive. But now, with my gray hair turning white, I've wanted to slow up.

Apparently, I haven't learned how.

Years ago, my wife and I vacationed in Mexico. We arrived at our beachside hotel, unpacked, and I immediately started looking for recreational activities. "See that thing," ordered Nancy. "It's a hammock. Lie in it!"

I did — following her direction because I long ago discovered the key to a happy marriage is a submissive "Yes, dear."

"What now?" I asked, squirming only slightly. "Now you lie there and stare at the ocean or the clouds in the sky. That's it."

"Yes, dear."

Within four minutes, I was uptight, upright, and looking for *active* recreational activities. I evidently don't do passive very well.

Still, to overcome my innate obsessive-compulsiveness, a condition amplified by being a Jew trapped in a Calvinist work ethic, I recently resolved as a follow-up to punch my pause-button for 24 hours.

I designated one Saturday as Do-Nothing Day, planning to completely veg out. I blueprinted it: Count tiny bumps in the ceiling while resting in bed. Listen to hours of soft, melodic, classic jazz. Watch lowbrow TV shows instead of anything on PBS that I might have to think about. Eat gobs of comfort food instead of low-fat this and extra-lite that.

I intended to travel a familiar road, the one paved with good intentions, but delete a few regular items along the way: No exercise. No errands. No phone calls.

But I failed. Utterly. Miserably. Swiftly.

Within four minutes of awakening, I was checking 13 bookmarked online news sites. Next up, stretching exercises, then the treadmill and recumbent bike. What followed — within half an hour — was making a phone call related to my chairmanship of an environmental commission; cell-phoning my daughter in New York; calling a friend to wish her a happy birthday; walking our dog and picking up his poop; helping my wife unclog a filing cabinet drawer; hauling a box filled with heavy paper to our storage shed; writing a cover letter to a literary agent; and crafting this column.

The rest of my day followed in kind, imitating most other 24-hour periods — crammed with limitless tasks with meaning for me even if nobody else gives a flying fig. But come to a full stop? Impossible. In fact, my Do-Nothing Day included a bit of "deferred maintenance," scrutinizing some 723 Post-its on my desk.

Years ago, I sold my Palm Pilot. I've never considered buying a Blackberry. Stickies are what I stick to. My desk, my pockets, my brain — each is jammed with them. They even ring my computer.

What do I scribble? Snippets of tidbits I've overhead. And sometimes my mind decides to become a giant sieve, with the best place for its drippings being those little yellow pieces of paper. Eventually, I do examine the squiggles, often actually able to decipher my handwriting.

Here are some recent notations:

- Damn! Can't lose weight! Why? With apologies to Will Rogers, I've never met a carb I didn't like.
- Little dark-haired girl about three in local park, obviously fighting off potential identity crisis: "I am *not* a sandcastle. I am *not* a sandcastle."
- Don't know why but the phrase "having some wiggle room" always makes me giggle.
- Woman overheard in front of a nearby musical hotspot while rubbing her wedding ring: "I fight with myself; why wouldn't I fight with my partner?"
- Clean your desk!
- Most ill-defined, overused word of the decade — "organic."
- Guy talking to two others in front of a market a few towns away: "He's so dumb, he couldn't fix a one-horse race."
- "Hot news" a couple of months back — 'Tanning salons cause cancer.' Duh!
- Cull the Post-its on desk! Today!
- Would anybody define "voyeur" as "having a peek experience"?
- Decked out female with blonde bangs at a supermarket in town, talking about husband's previous spouse: "He did that in another *wife*time."
- I'm such an optimist I think a bad start almost inevitably leads to a good finish.

- Would-be political candidate talking to would-be voter, sez, "I don't have a 'for sale' sign on my back."
- Handful of environmental purists irk me by acting as if they're greener than thou.

But by far the most significant Post-it I uncovered, one that instantly got me to stop whipping myself for my Do-Nothing Day fiasco, was: Overheard on lawn not far from home — "I took a lot of baby steps this week, *most* of them forward."

Short autobiography of the author

I can't remember when I couldn't talk — or play with words.

My first poem was published in high school, but when my hormones screamed that adulthood had arrived, I decided I'd rather eat than create rhymes (or even blank verse). So, I switched to journalism, jumpstarting my career in New Yawk more than 60 years ago.

Now I'm a feature writer, critic/reviewer, blogger, and publisher — despite allegedly being retired.

For many years, I was volunteer chair of the environmentally sensitive Quality of Life Commission in my adopted hometown, San Anselmo, California, and a member of the Marin County Commission on Aging, a Supervisor-appointed position.

During my earlier, better-paid years as a wage-slave, I was an executive editor and writer for daily and weekly publications in California, Florida, New Jersey, Pennsylvania, and New York for five decades.

I won writing awards for public service and investigation, features, columns, editorials, and news.

In collaboration with my wife, Nancy Fox, heroine of my first book, *Rollercoaster: How a man can survive his partner's breast cancer*, I completed an original musical revue, *Touching Up the Gray*. We're still waiting patiently for a Broadway producer to miraculously appear.

As an outgrowth of my long-term caregiving, I've led — for almost 30 years — a weekly support group for men whose mates had life-threatening diseases.

Now an octogenarian whose previous spouse died after her breast cancer spread to vital organs, I've also published newspapers and written a national column for *Audio* magazine. In addition, I collaborated with my then 8-year-old granddaughter, Hannah Schifrin, on a children's fantasy book, *Grampy and His Fairyzona Playmates.*

A graduate of Colgate University, I owned a public relations/ad agency, directed a congressional primary campaign, served as media liaison for a psychiatric hospital, managed an advertising publication, and worked as a legislative aide.

The father of two and grandfather of three, I've lived in San Anselmo for more than 35 years.

I figure I'll stay.

www.ingramcontent.com/pod-product-compliance
Lightning Source LLC
Chambersburg PA
CBHW060941120726
47910CB00002B/439

* 9 7 8 0 9 9 0 5 5 4 3 6 3 *